Avidly Reads

General Editor: Sarah Mesle

Founding Editors: Sarah Blackwood and Sarah Mesle

The Avidly Reads series presents brief books about how culture makes us feel. We invite readers and writers to indulge feelings—and to tell their stories—in the idiom that distinguishes the best conversations about culture.

Avidly Reads Theory
Jordan Alexander Stein

Avidly Reads Board Games
Eric Thurm

Avidly Reads Making Out
Kathryn Bond Stockton

Avidly Reads Passages
Michelle D. Commander

Avidly Reads Guilty Pleasures
Arielle Zibrak

Avidly Reads Opera
Alison Kinney

Avidly Reads Poetry
Jacquelyn Ardam

Poetry

JACQUELYN ARDAM

NEW YORK UNIVERSITY PRESS *New York*

NEW YORK UNIVERSITY PRESS
New York
www.nyupress.org

© 2022 by New York University
All rights reserved

References to Internet websites (URLs) were accurate at the time of writing. Neither the author nor New York University Press is responsible for URLs that may have expired or changed since the manuscript was prepared.

Cataloging-in-Publication data is available from the publisher.

9781479813551 (hardback)
9781479813582 (paperback)
9781479813605 (library ebook)
9781479813612 (consumer ebook)

New York University Press books are printed on acid-free paper, and their binding materials are chosen for strength and durability. We strive to use environmentally responsible suppliers and materials to the greatest extent possible in publishing our books.

Manufactured in the United States of America

10 9 8 7 6 5 4 3 2 1

Also available as an ebook

For my parents,

Diane and David Ardam

Contents

Introduction   1

1 The Sonnet: To Want   15

2 The Alphabet Poem: To Learn   47

3 The Documentary Poem: To Resist   77

4 The Internet Poem: To Soothe   113

Coda: The Villanelle: To Lose   147

Acknowledgments   153

Works Cited and Consulted   157

About the Author   161

INTRODUCTION

Not very long ago, I moved from Los Angeles to central Maine for a job teaching poetry. The decision could be hard to explain. My new dentist, for instance, with her hands deep inside my mouth, asked, "Do people still read poetry? I had no idea." I pointed at myself, attempted a smile, and shrugged. My dentist changed the subject.

I spent years listening to the reasons why people don't read poems. Poems are cheesy and boring. Reading poems is something you do in high school and then never again. Poems try to trick you with their secret meanings. They are obscure and purposefully dense. Poems are written by dead white men, or by sad emo teenage girls, and who would want to spend time with either? Poems do nothing except offer opportunities for smugness to self-consciously weird people in berets who like to go to poetry readings with their weird smug friends.

But something has changed.

When you devote a life to something peripheral—like I did, with poetry—and you are told over and over again that it is peripheral by the people whom you love, or teach, or whose hands are in your mouth,

1

it can be a strange thing to exist in a changed world, where poetry, it suddenly seems, is everywhere. Poetry sales have skyrocketed in the past decade. The genre has become one of the fastest-growing categories in the publishing industry. *Dickinson*, a show about the nineteenth-century American poet, is a major hit on Apple TV+. Khloé Kardashian regularly shares poems with her 189 million followers on her Instagram account. At Joe Biden's inauguration in 2021, Amanda Gorman, a young Black woman and the first national youth poet laureate, performed her poem "The Hill We Climb" and the nation watched in awe. The poem, which acknowledged the country's garbage past but remained hopeful for a better future, drew upon America's Black poetic history, incorporating influences from Langston Hughes to Maya Angelou to spoken-word poetry. Then Amanda Gorman performed at the 2021 Super Bowl. At the Super Bowl! Her profound influence on US culture is enough to convince me that in 2021, poetry, just like I always thought it could be, is for everyone.

I may have grown up in a time when poetry seemed to be this rarefied thing, only for the smug and elite, but this wasn't how poetry was always seen in the United States. Nineteenth-century Americans printed, circulated, exchanged, and memorized poetry; it was part of daily life. It's not surprising that the poet considered by many to be the quintessential American poet—Walt Whitman—wrote poems that were big, accessible, and inclusive, and addressed to the broadest possible American poetry-reading public. Whitman wasn't so well-known during his lifetime, but he truly did celebrate democracy and American bodies alongside each other, always emphasizing the interconnectedness of all people, writing famously in "Song of Myself" that "every atom belonging to me as good belongs to you." He wrote poems in free verse, and he loved a good list, often enumerating all of the different types of Americans, and inviting us all to "loafe with [him] on the grass" and see America for what it was: the best. (It was not the best, and nor was he, but we will get to that later.) For Whitman, America's body politic was sensuous and earthly; he famously wrote that the "United States themselves are essentially the greatest poem," a delicious poem that he certainly would have fucked if he could. "I am the mate and companion of people," he wrote. It is this expansive vision of nineteenth-century America, in which poetry (and the poet himself) is for everyone, that persists from Whitman's poems.

Before I knew anything about Walt Whitman the poet, I knew about Walt Whitman the mall. I grew up near Whitman's birthplace on Long Island and spent many formative years at the mall named for him, a mall like any other mall in America, a place for indolent teens and little old ladies with walkers and everyone in between who wanted to delight in an Auntie Anne's pretzel. In my imagination, Whitman loves his mall, because the mall is a space for everyone. But by the time I started reading poetry in middle school in the 1990s, poetry felt different. The actual nineteenth-century poetry-reading public and Whitman's romantic vision of it no longer existed. In the 1990s, poetry felt like something crystalline and delicate. Something that might give me access to some kind of secret society or literary elite, which I wanted to be a part of, though I didn't have the language for that at the time.

When I first read Whitman in college, we talked about his expansive and sensual embrace of all Americans and I felt embraced by him. It was not until graduate school that I learned to complicate my understanding of the poet and his American past. Whitman didn't actually love everyone in this country; I read his poems that characterized Native peoples as savages, which rendered their genocide as progress for white people. I read scholarly articles about his racism, a racism that I, in my ignorance, did not see when I first read his poems at nineteen. Racism has been a part of American poetry as long as there has been American poetry. This is not news, of course; anti-racism has also been a part of American poetry as long as there has been American poetry, and poets of color have long reckoned with the question of who gets to count in an American "everyone." But something has shifted over the course of my adult life. Conversations about race and poetry are being had by more people, and at a higher volume, than they were when I started studying poetry.

These conversations are not limited to classrooms and scholarly journals. The increasing visibility of poetry in the public sphere has been accompanied by an increased attention to the relationship between poetry and white supremacy.

A moment from a few years ago, I think, captures the shift perfectly. I will set the scene. It is November 9, 2015, and then–presidential candidate Donald Trump is spewing racist garbage at a campaign rally in Springfield, Illinois. The event is streaming, and visible behind Trump at a podium is a diverse group of people sitting on risers. This group includes a young Black woman who is conspicuously reading a book. The woman, Johari Osayi Idusuyi, opens the book midway through the rally, eventually holding it up high in front of her face. An older white couple watches Idusuyi reading, and the man leans over and taps her on the shoulder, gestures at the book, and appears to chastise her for not paying attention to Trump. Idusuyi looks surprised, speaks to the man, and then turns back to her book, once again holding it up high, making it visible to anyone watching the rally from home. The book is poet Claudia Rankine's *Citizen: An American Lyric.*

Certain corners of the internet go wild over the next twenty-four hours. At this moment I am new to Twitter, which is where I learn about Idusuyi, and I watch the moment unfold with pleasure. I love when poetry goes viral. The moment is soon covered in all sorts of media. *Jezebel*'s headline that night reads

"We Are All This Woman Refusing to Put Down Her Book at a Trump Rally." NPR reports on the story. Idusuyi is mentioned on *Jimmy Kimmel Live*, on *BET News*, in *Business Insider*, on the *Huffington Post*. A few days after the rally, Rachel Maddow interviews Idusuyi on her show and wants to discuss both the campaign event and Rankine's *Citizen*. In the buildup to the interview, Maddow positions herself as an outsider to poetry. She claims that "I don't know exactly how that [poetry] world works" and smiles sheepishly in acknowledgement that it really is silly to be talking about poetry on a cable news show. Maddow explains that *Citizen* is about "everyday experiences of racism in the United States" and says that "in that world"—in other words, in the poetry world—*Citizen* is "a big deal." (I can confirm: it was, and is, a big deal.)

In her interview with Idusuyi, Maddow wants to know how this young woman—not exactly the prototypical Trump supporter—came to be sitting behind Trump in the first place (a friend had extra tickets and she was curious), how she felt about Trump's remarks (disgusted), and whether she planned to vote for him (no). Maddow notes that by the end of the televised rally, Trump supporters are waving large Trump signs; Idusuyi is waving her copy of *Citizen*. In this viral moment, which Maddow digests for her audience as a form of protest against Trump, poetry has crept out of its world and into *the* world. But for Idusuyi, these disparate worlds seem less distinct.

She is the woman—the reader—who, she explains, brought what she just happened to be reading to a political rally in case she ended up waiting in a lot of long lines.

In fact, Idusuyi explains to several journalists that her reading poetry at a Trump rally was not a planned protest. It was just something she did, as one does, when one reads poetry. And I got it; I too, am someone who carries books of poetry in her purse in case she gets bored, a fact that has not gone un-commented upon by the non–poetry readers in my life. In an interview with *Jezebel*, Idusuyi talks about being turned off by Trump's hateful comments about a protester at the rally and explains, "And that's when I was like, I am now genuinely not interested in your speech. I wanted to leave, but I came, I'm in the mid-dle, I'm on camera, so I might as well read because I don't have anything else to do. I'm not going to waste my time listening to somebody who I can't respect anymore, so I started to read."

"For women, poetry is not a luxury," the Black feminist thinker and poet Audre Lorde famously writes in a 1977 essay: "It is a vital necessity of our existence." Lorde's "our" specifically addresses Black women, but I think that her sentiment appeals to a broad swath of others too. Many Americans—and all indications point to a growing number of Americans—live an existence in which poetry is not a discrete supplement to the world, but a vital experience in and of it. Idusuyi is reading *Citizen* not as a way of escaping the world, but as a way of living. This is the premise of this book: that poetry is not a luxury, that poetry matters in the twenty-first century.

Idusuyi may not have planned to read *Citizen* in an act of defiance of Trump, but it is important that the moment was read by many others as a form of political protest. The image of a young Black woman sharing the screen with Trump, diverting attention from him, overtaking his media coverage, and quietly yet powerfully disavowing him by reading a book of poetry about racism electrified so many. And for those of us who have read Rankine's *Citizen*, and know that it is a book that redefines the lyric—the genre of poetry often characterized by a solitary speaker, like Whitman, addressing a "you"—by collapsing speaker and addressee in on themselves, the moment is almost too good to be true. So much of *Citizen* is about questions of audience—who is speaking, whose "I" can claim to speak as a citizen, who is being addressed when Rankine writes to "you"—and Idusuyi's act of reading when in audience to Trump amplifies Rankine's concerns about voice, race, and poetic address. It makes me want to ask Idusuyi so many questions about herself and her experience reading the book: why *Citizen*? How does it address you? What were you hoping to find within its pages, and what did you find there? What does it articulate for you or teach you? How do you see yourself in poems? What did *Citizen* do for you, as a person, not a symbol, while you had a literal front row seat to Trump's racism?

These are the types of questions I seek to answer in this book, not on behalf of Idusuyi, but for a larger US public engaged with reading poems anew. How did we move from Idusuyi reading quietly behind Trump in 2015 to Amanda Gorman reading in front of a newly elected Biden in 2021? When Rankine writes "you," when Gorman says "we," who is included? Who is addressed?

* * *

I was once a poetry professor, and my whole life revolved around those two things: poetry, and being a professor. That ended in 2019. Though I still work at a university in an administrator role, poetry is no longer the center of my life as it once was. The shift in my career has been difficult for me in many ways, some of which I discuss in this book, but it has also been a chance for me to think about poetry anew and outside the often narrow parameters of academic scholarship. In this transitional moment in my life, it has been interesting to chart both my changed relationship with my former object of study and poetry's increasing visibility in the public sphere. Poetry and I, we are on a journey together.

I have spent so much of my life thinking about poetry in an academic way: about poetic traditions and histories, about how one poet responds or relates to another, about theories of poetry, about methods of interpreting poetry, about aesthetic movements, about what this or that critic thinks (and whether I agree with them), about what I think is important for my students and my academic peers to know. I have spent a lot of time telling people what they should think about poetry. I know a lot about it! It was my job! But now that my ideas about poetry are no longer tied to the way I get health insurance, I find myself in a different position, able to ask different questions than I might have asked in the past.

In writing this book, I have kept some of the approaches to reading and critiquing poetry that I learned in my academic training and I have let others go. And it was hard to let them go; I lost a career in poetry, but I didn't lose my training or the (yes, pretty gross) sense of superiority that you get when you are an expert in something that not many people are an expert in. Poetry was for a long time My Thing, and I can still feel possessive about it. But if I think poetry is for everyone—and I really do think that—I have to evaluate poetry differently and I have to ask bigger, broader questions than I did before. It's clear that more people are reading poetry and I want to know why and how. How do poems come to us? How do they make us feel and think and act when they do? Who and what is poetry for? Who does poetry include and exclude, and what can we learn from it?

What can *I* learn from it, if I want to hold both my expertise and my newer needs in hand?

The book begins in September 2001, my first month of college, and looks backward to the 1990s. It ends in 2021, with the COVID-19 pandemic. Throughout this arc of time, which is also the arc of my adulthood, the United States has undergone seismic changes that have both nothing and everything to do with poetry. In this time period, the country has, slowly, and with much resistance and vicious backlash, reevaluated and challenged its cultural institutions, including its valuation of the many dead white men of America's past. In the 2010s, we saw the rise of Trump and the reentrenchment of white supremacy in the political sphere. At the same time, poetry readers around the country challenged the myth of the white male genius arbiter of culture, the myth of Whitman and his brethren. I do not think these shifts are unrelated.

The day after Trump's election, when I was teaching a modern American poetry class at a small college in Maine, I tossed out whatever I had assigned that day on the syllabus and brought in Langston Hughes's "Let America Be America Again," a poem first published in 1936 that to me felt imperative to read not just as a rejoinder to the general white supremacist fantasies of America, but to Trump specifically. In the poem's title, I hear a foreshadowing of Trump's "Make America Great Again" slogan. In the poem, Hughes writes:

Let America be the dream the dreamers dreamed—

Let it be that great strong land of love
Where never kings connive nor tyrants scheme
That any man be crushed by one above.

(It never was America to me.)

The mythic America, which Whitman believed in and helped create, is not an America for all. Through the haunting refrain—"America never was America for me"—which repeats with small differences throughout the poem, Hughes insists that the white experience of America is not universal, that America will never be what it has long promised it is until "equality is in the air we breathe" and "*every* man is free." Every time Trump says "Make America Great Again," and he is still saying it, I reflexively remember the end of Hughes's poem:

O, yes,
I say it plain,
America never was America to me,
And yet I swear this oath—
America will be!

Out of the rack and ruin of our gangster death,
The rape and rot of graft, and stealth, and lies,
We, the people, must redeem
The land, the mines, the plants, the rivers.

The mountains and the endless plain—
All, all the stretch of these great green states—
And make America again!

We do not, as Trump says, need to make America great again. As Hughes says, we need to "make America again." We need to make it over.

Of course, there are no redos to history. We can never make America over. But poetry provides a space for those of us who want to ask: how might we make it better? Or, to quote Amanda Gorman, we are "a nation that isn't broken but simply unfinished"—"we will not march back to what was, / but move to what shall be." Hughes's and Gorman's poems have an expectation about America that I admire. They demand that it be better. I don't know if I can muster hope that their demands will be met, given my general disposition and the atrocities of late capitalism (my love for the mall notwithstanding), America's imperialism, the white supremacy, the income inequality, the mass incarceration, the mass shootings, the destruction of our climate, the millions of COVID-19 deaths worldwide, just to name a few things that are on my mind. But still, I find myself reading Hughes, and still, I find myself watching Gorman's inaugural reading. Poetry has become less peripheral in my lifetime, but poetry has long been the space for those on many kinds of peripheries to encounter our individual and political selves.

This book asks why we turn to poetry when we do—why we might be carrying a copy of *Citizen* in our purses at a campaign rally or scrolling through the @poetryisnotaluxury Instagram account on our phones with our morning coffee. In each section, I link a reason why we might read poetry (to want, to learn, to resist, to soothe) with a type of poem (the sonnet, the alphabet poem, the documentary poem, the internet poem). Through readings of poems written in English from the early modern era through today, and through reading the American cultures in which we read them, I think about how poems are embedded in our lives: in our loves, our educations, our politics, and our social media, sometimes in spite of, and sometimes very much because of the country we live in.

1

THE SONNET

To Want

Being a teenager is about wanting, which is why sonnets are such an ideal form for teenagers. In the 1990s, when I was a teen, there was a mini-boom of sonnets in American popular media that marked a meeting of high and low culture that I didn't quite appreciate at the time. I was young and self-centered and white, and the fact that teen pop culture seemed directed exactly toward me, a me who had spent seventh grade memorizing sonnets by Shakespeare in English class, seemed right and natural rather than surprising. The sonnets that appeared in the movies and television that I loved spoke to me, and I happily saw myself in the teen girls—Julia Stiles, Claire Danes—who spoke them. At the time, I had no idea that a sonnet could be for anything other than wanting someone, and wanting them to want you back.

The sonnet is *the* form of forms; it is so ubiquitous that it is often a synecdoche for poetry itself. Many of the canonized heavy hitters of English poetry—William Shakespeare, John Donne, John Milton, William Wordsworth, John Keats, to name a few—

wrote sonnets. These were the dead white men who I learned about in college, the men who explained to me what Serious Poetry is. Yet I had a very different experience of sonnets in the 1990s, as they kept appearing in the teen films and television shows that I watched again and again. Before I knew anything scholarly about sonnets at all, I knew that they were a way to get what you wanted when what you wanted was a boy.

When I was in high school, I wanted a lot of things. I wanted boys to like me and I had a lot of ideas about why and how they should like me. (On the whole, they did not like me, at least, not in "that way.") I wanted them to see that I was different from other girls, and, like, intellectual, but for sure in a pretty way. I also wanted other things: to get off of Long Island and leave the suburbs forever, to go to a "good college," but that wasn't the same sort of wanting for me. It was institutional, social. Going to a "good college" always felt within the realm of possibilities; it was something I could make happen with good grades (which I got) and privilege (which I had). More intimate forms of wanting were harder. Liking boys didn't pan out for me so well in high school, so as a young person I came to understand myself as a wanter, not a haver. I felt myself on some periphery, despite my abundant privilege, and I held this belief about myself for a long time. From the vantage point of my late thirties, my young self seems incredibly sad and anxious, but in my late teens, I felt very romantic (in addition, I suppose, to feeling very sad and anxious). I didn't know any better and I thought my yearning was extremely beautiful.

I started college in the fall of 2001, right before the world changed, and before what people wanted poetry to do in the world changed. At eighteen, I could not have imagined the political turmoil of the coming years, nor how poetry would respond to it. Poetry was all yearning for me then, and during my college orientation in August, I signed up for a creative writing poetry class because I yearned. I liked the idea of writing poetry and being good at it and being the type of person who *would* write poetry, the type of girl who would attract "artsy" guys because I was, like, deep and maybe a bit weird, but again, in a pretty way, and maybe these guys would be in my poetry class.

I showed up to my first poetry class and it turned out the class was small and the professor was dreamy and had thick beautiful hair. We read so many good poems and we wrote pretty terrible ones. One boy kept writing bad poems about his green lighter. I suspected he wrote his poems quickly in the moments before they were due, while I labored over my short bad poems for many hours. I harbored the deepest crush imaginable on my professor and his thick dark hair. One week, the professor told our class that everyone writes sonnets, that they are literally universal, that if there are aliens on another planet, for sure they are writing sonnets.

For class the next week I wrote a sonnet. It was fourteen lines long and it didn't rhyme and I didn't capitalize any letters (not even "i"). The sonnet was about eating oranges and looking at the moon. September 11 had just happened, so of course I wrote a sonnet about eating oranges and looking at the moon; the world had changed but it hadn't, yet, changed me. At some point while we were work-shopping the poem, the professor said, "Well, this is clearly a sex poem," and so I died. I had not yet had sex at that point in my life, and the thought that I, a wanter, not a haver, could unknowingly write a sex sonnet that was identified as such by this beauti-ful thick-haired man was both the most wonderful and horrifying thing that had ever happened to me. I burned, and then I wrote a lot of other poems about oranges for many years.

* * *

Why does everyone write sonnets? I have some ideas. The first is that everyone writes them because every-one has for more than seven hundred years. The pull of history is strong. But also, despite that long time frame, sonnets are short. In the time it might take you to write a one-hundred-line poem, you might be able to get in a solid seven or so sonnets. This is not a joke; I think their brevity is key to their popularity. And sonnets are some of the first poems many of us read in middle or high school outside of the (admit-tedly loosey-goosey) category of children's literature.

But the standard themes of sonnets are important too: sonnets are often, if not always, about wanting and desire, and those are topics that resonate with many people. Maybe everyone. When I was young, I didn't realize that you could write about wanting things other than boys; I had no idea about the sonnet traditions that I will discuss later that have to do with political sorts of wanting and how intimate that, too, can feel. I wrote sonnets because a man with great hair told me it was the thing to do, and I wrote sonnets about wanting boys because that is what my popular media told me sonnets were for. Does it need to be said that I was an extremely basic straight white cis teenage girl who thought that she wasn't? Because I most definitely was.

In high school I loved the film *10 Things I Hate about You* (1999) and I still do. The movie can tell us a lot about sonnets: about teen girls (actual teen girls, as well as the figure of the "teen girl") and desire, about why we write poems and for whom, about what we hope we might find in poems, including ourselves. It is one of the many 1990s movies and television shows that uses poetry—and in particular, Shakespeare's sonnets—as an occasion for teen discovery. I am not the first to note that Shakespeare loomed large in this pop cultural moment, but it has always struck me that there is something curious about the association of Shakespeare, the Most Important Writer of All Time with . . . teenage girls? How did a towering cultural figure, a long-dead figure of erudition and sophistication, become so associated in the 1990s with fifteen-year-old alt-girls in flannel? Who could be more important and who could be less?

To be clear, nothing is more interesting to me than the feelings of teenage girls. But American culture has long had a way of being interested in them only pruriently and only as a fantasy of themselves, and when they are white and conventionally attractive and ideally blonde, and possibly dead. But in this cultural moment, Shakespeare and white teenage girls had a few years of pop cultural alignment. Shakespeare himself, embodied by the delicious Joseph Fiennes, became a figure of desire—a figure of ardent wanting as well as the object of Gwyneth's desire—in the 1998 film *Shakespeare in Love*. And teen girls, and particularly a certain brand of white alt-teen girls, played similar roles in television and films. In this moment, the Shakespearean sonnet was a medium through which they could be both desiring subject and desired object. We were used to seeing teen girls as objects of others' desires; through Shakespeare's sonnets in film and on TV, they could also be subjects who wanted.

Sonnets have been about wanting since their beginning. Petrarch, the Italian poet who popularized the form in the fourteenth century, wrote about unrequited love. His sonnets feature a male speaker addressing a woman, Laura, whom he wants but who remains elusive. She is a beautiful but cold ice queen, uninterested in the speaker's professions of love. Shakespeare, meanwhile, dedicated his sequence of 154 sonnets to a "Mr. W. H." and addressed the first 126 of them to a young man known as the "Fair Youth." While we may not know if this Fair Youth was indeed Mr. W. H., we do know that he was hot. The speaker of Shakespeare's poems spends a lot of time urging him to find a wife so that he can have children and reproduce his beauty in the world while the poet immortalizes him in poetry. The Dark Lady sonnets that follow the Fair Youth sonnets are sexier, darker; in these poems, the speaker finds himself in a love triangle with the Fair Youth and the Dark Lady. It's this legacy of wanting, from Petrarch on through Shakespeare, that *10 Things I Hate about You* receives and refits for its teenage viewers. The sonnet is a way of articulating want for a person or, as we will see later, a form for other sorts of wanting, including wanting political change.

What is most important about the sonnet's structure, its way of sorting through want and want's complexities, is its volta. When I teach sonnets, I frame them for my students as tiny thought experiments. The beginning of a sonnet often sets out an idea via a declarative statement, or a question, or a hypothetical scenario. Then there is a turn of some sort in the poem. This turn is the "volta." The poem changes course in some way, and the sonnet introduces a different idea, or a contradiction, or a reassessment. It answers a question, or reaches a deeper level of understanding. Shakespeare's sonnets rarely end where they begin. In his day, the sonnet (usually) consisted of fourteen lines of iambic pentameter, and Shakespeare ended his sonnets with a rhyming couplet. Often, this couplet brought, with its new rhyme scheme, a volta. Shakespeare used these poems as ways of thinking through and arriving somewhere new, forms of arguing with one's self, forms of realization and revelation. And often these revelations are about wanting: who and what and when one wants. And sometimes why. And often how.

* * *

In *10 Things I Hate about You*, Mr. Morgan, an English teacher at Padua High, gives the students in his class a homework assignment to rewrite Shakespeare's Sonnet 141. Mr. Morgan is a cool English teacher, or is at least trying to be one, so he raps the first four lines of the poem to the class:

> In faith, I do not love thee with mine eyes,
> For they in thee a thousand errors note;
> But 'tis my heart that loves what they despise,
> Who, in despite of view is pleased to dote;

This is not one of Shakespeare's more tender sonnets. No one is comparing anyone to a summer's day here. This sonnet is both a monumental diss of a poem—you're not cute and there are a thousand things wrong with you—and a monument to the speaker's desire. The speaker despises the Dark Lady, but as the poem goes on, we find out that he needs her and that he enjoys the pain that she causes him. It's all a bit emo.

Kat Stratford (played by Julia Stiles), a student in Mr. Morgan's class, is really into the sonnet-rewriting assignment. She enthusiastically asks her teacher if he wants the poem to be written in iambic pentameter, showing she really knows her high culture. When Mr. Morgan accuses her of being snarky, Kat says, "No, I think it's a really good assignment," and then, earnestly, "I'm really looking forward to writing it." Attributing irony where there is none, Mr. Morgan kicks her out of class. (This is not good pedagogy.) Kat has a reputation, you see. She is a young feminist; she listens to all-girl bands, she (mostly) doesn't wear makeup, she is smart and funny, she sees through and is dismissive of all kinds of male nonsense. She wants to go to Sarah Lawrence for college. Unfortunately, she has also fallen in love, and falling in love will become the avenue for her to integrate her outsider Riot Grrrl–ish status into the established paradigm of the teen romance.

10 Things I Hate about You, which was directed by Gil Junger, retells Shakespeare's The Taming of the Shrew. In the film, Kat has fallen for a rakish outsider, Patrick Verona, played by Heath Ledger, who, because this is an adaptation of a Shakespeare comedy, has been paid to go out with Kat by another boy who actually wants to date Kat's younger sister, who

can only date if Kat is dating. Kat doesn't know any of this though, and Kat, who is hostile to most boys (and for good reason), is slowly won over by Patrick, who has great hair, and who is also slowly, and in spite of himself, won over by Kat. They fall for each other over several scenes including an extremely charming song-and-dance number by Patrick on the football field risers as well as a flirty paintball game. When Kat ultimately finds out the truth behind Patrick's pursuit of her, she is devastated. At the prom.

Cut to English class, some time after the prom. Mr. Morgan asks if anyone is brave enough to share their sonnet homework assignment. Kat volunteers. The camera cuts to Patrick, who has what can only be described as an "oh shit" look on his face. Kat walks to the front of the classroom holding a three-ring binder. She reads:

> I hate the way you talk to me
> And the way you cut your hair
> I hate the way you drive my car
> I hate it when you stare
>
> I hate your big dumb combat boots
> And the way you read my mind
> I hate you so much that it makes me sick
> It even makes me rhyme.

At this line, Kat raises her eyebrows a bit and acknowledges the silliness of the rhyme. The camera begins to zoom in on Kat, and she stumbles just a bit over the next line of the poem. She says:

> I hate it—I hate the way you're always right
> I hate it when you lie
> I hate it when you make me laugh
> Even worse when you make me cry

Throughout her performance, she has been tentatively looking in the direction of Patrick. Now, she is looking straight at him. The camera is tight to her face. Kat tears up, and her voice begins to waver:

> I hate the way you're not around
> And the fact that you didn't call
> But mostly I hate the way I don't hate you
> Not even close, not even a little bit, not even at all.

The camera cuts to Patrick. He is sitting at his desk with his hands clasped in front of his face. The camera cuts back to Kat; she is crying and walks quickly out of the classroom. The camera lingers on Patrick and cheesy orchestral music begins to swell. Kat's message—I hate you, but actually I love you—has been received.

The film ends moments later with our main characters in the school parking lot. Patrick has bought Kat a Fender guitar as an apology and as an attempt to win her back. He explains: "Some asshole paid me to take out this really great girl, but I screwed up, I fell for her."

They kiss, and then they banter wittily between kisses. A cover of the Cheap Trick song "I Want You to Want Me" plays. The camera pans out from Kat and Patrick making out in the parking lot and cuts to a long slow aerial shot of the band Letters to Cleo performing the song on the school roof. The outsiders have been brought in; the counterculture has been perfectly commodified. The credits begin to roll. It is so perfectly nineties that today it almost hurts to watch.

* * *

To understand Kat's sonnet within the long sonnet tradition, let's look at Shakespeare's Sonnet 141, which is addressed to the Dark Lady, in full:

> In faith, I do not love thee with mine eyes,
> For they in thee a thousand errors note;
> But 'tis my heart that loves what they despise,
> Who, in despite of view is pleased to dote;
> Nor are mine ears with thy tongue's tune
>   delighted,
> Nor tender feeling to base touches prone,
> Nor taste, nor smell, desire to be invited
> To any sensual feast with thee alone:
> But my five wits nor my five senses can
> Dissuade one foolish heart from serving thee,
> Who leaves unswayed the likeness of a man,
> Thy proud heart's slave and vassal wretch to be:
> Only my plague thus far I count my gain,
> That she that makes me sin, awards me pain.

The octave, the first eight lines of the sonnet, begins with one set of ideas: I do not like the look of you and there are a thousand things wrong with you, but my heart loves you. In the sestet, the next six lines of the sonnet, the speaker stops talking about love and things get kinky. He figures himself as the Dark Lady's servant, and then cranks that metaphor up a notch and suggests he is her "slave and vassal wretch." The poem begins with opposing and ambivalent feelings: I hate you and I love you! But in the sestet, the ambivalent feelings become more complex; the speaker realizes that hate and love are not opposed but intrinsic to one another. This sestet is sadomasochistic and the Dark Lady is on top. At the end of the poem, she "awards" the speaker a "plague" as well as "pain." We can read the "plague" figuratively as a kind of lovesickness within a sadomasochistic relationship, or more literally as venereal disease. This is a poem that has fucked.

In rewriting Shakespeare's Sonnet 141, Kat places herself in a long line of sonneteers who make and remake the form. Her performance of her sonnet is a turning point in the plot of the film, and though she doesn't announce the poem's title when she reads it in front of the class, the title of the film (*10 Things I Hate about You*) is the implied title of the poem. Kat's sonnet is worth reading closely, both for how it interacts with Shakespeare and for its centrality in the film's plot. The first thing that we should note is that Kat takes many liberties with her class assignment.

Her poem is not written in iambic pentameter. It has sixteen, not fourteen lines, and it doesn't end with a signature Shakespearean couplet.

Sonnet purists might argue that Kat's classroom assignment is not indeed a sonnet because it doesn't have fourteen lines. I have never been a critic who wants to argue about whether or not something is a sonnet if the author says it is a sonnet. Instead, I ask: what does Kat accomplish by writing within the sonnet tradition? When we look at Kat's poem and Shakespeare's Sonnet 141 alongside each other, we realize that in some ways it is a faithful revision. Kat, like Shakespeare, makes a list. She "hates" Patrick's combat boots, his lying, his (extremely cute shaggy) hair, and so on. Kat's sonnet, like Shakespeare's, relies on anaphora, or the repetition of a phrase at the beginning of successive lines of poetry: Shakespeare's "nor"s become Kat's "I hate"s. Shakespeare's syntax is much more complex than Kat's, but the ideas are the same: here are all of the things I hate about you. I suspect that Kat might also be referencing the poem of another sonneteer, Elizabeth Barrett Browning, whose Sonnet 43 famously begins "How do I love thee? Let me count the ways," which is another litany of love organized by anaphora.

But Kat's poem is revealed to be the love poem that we suspected it might be only at its end. Her sonnet has a volta—a very late volta—at line 15. After listing all of the things that she hates about Patrick, she declares, "But mostly I hate the way I don't hate you / Not even close, not even a little bit, not even at all." All of her repeated declarations of hate have been, in fact, the repetition of an untruth: her declarations of hate might more accurately be interpreted as declarations of love. The "ten things" Kat hates about Patrick are not in fact things that she hates about him at all (really, who *could* hate the hair?). It also seems worth noting that depending on what we count as a discrete "thing" (a philosophical can of worms to be sure) there are more like twelve things Kat hates about Patrick in her poem. But no matter. Kat's list of ten things contains twelve things, her sonnet contains sixteen lines; she is an avant-gardist and she contains multitudes.

Kat's poem does an about-face in her volta, which allows us to see she has been lying to herself. This is not a poem about hate; it's been a poem about how we deceive ourselves in matters of the heart. She has loved him all along! But what Kat has left out are the ways in which hate and love, pain and pleasure, might be sexily intertwined. Kat's poem operates on a kind of binary logic which Shakespeare's original work refuses. Shakespeare's volta reveals the coexistence of hate and love; Kat's volta reveals love not hate. Kat's poem loves; Shakespeare's poem fucks.

Or, to frame things less crassly: Kat's sonnet is very much the sonnet of a nineties white teenage girl, which is to say that her sonnet fits in the genre of the teen comedy, or even the (Shakespearean) comedy writ large, which is all about wanting and not having.

The wanting-and-not-having trope of teenagerness is both a cultural construct of teenagerness and true to my own experience. I fit right in. The moment that a character has what she wants is the moment the play or movie ends; the credits of *10 Things I Hate about You* are rolling within five minutes of Kat's reading of her poem. Her sonnet performs an important social function; it is an occasion for her both to realize (at the volta) and to express what she wants. It is also, crucially, an occasion for Kat to *get* what she wants: an apology from Patrick, a Fender guitar, and a conciliatory makeout in a school parking lot. Kat's sonnet makes things happen, but once they do happen, the film is over.

When the camera pans up and out to reveal Letters to Cleo playing "I Want You to Want Me" on the roof of Padua High, what we have is a perfect encapsulation of the teen comedy that ends with a kiss: a suspended state in which you get what you want, which is that the person you want wants you back. (Sarah Lawrence and the end of the patriarchy are, in the moment, backburnered.) The film ends in a moment of reciprocity, sparked by the revelations of the sonnet: I want you to want me and you do! In this, Kat's sonnet is much more akin to the first 126 sonnets in Shakespeare's sequence that are addressed to the Fair Youth, in which love is never consummated. Once the Dark Lady enters the picture, and desire is very much consummated, Shakespeare's sonnets become much less about wanting and much more about the ravages of having. Sex complicates things. The stakes get bigger.

* * *

There was not a lot of nuance in the wanting of the teens that I watched on television and in movies in the 1990s. Their feelings were big and all-consuming and they could turn on a dime. Or a sonnet. On *My So-Called Life*, Angela Chase (Claire Danes) yearns for Jordan Catalano (Jared Leto) magnificently. At the beginning of the show, which aired for just one perfect season on ABC from 1994 to 1995, and which I watched in reruns on MTV a few years later, Angela's crush on Jordan Catalano is unrequited, deep, and true. It is a yearning that feels particularly accurate to me in its scope and its intensity, and I can never quite tell if that's because that's just how teens are, or because something about Angela hit particularly close to home with me. Did I crush because that is what teenagers do, or because Angela Chase taught me how? Did I learn from the show that the crusher is always infinitely more interesting than the crushee, and did I cling to that insight for years? (Yes.)

Jordan is quiet, inarticulate, and dreamy. His eyes are big and expressive, and his hair is long and soft. He is the fairest of fair youths. He and Angela stumble toward each other in fits and starts, and by midseason, they are making out in the high school boiler room. But Jordan isn't as into Angela as she is into him. He doesn't want to acknowledge that anything is going on between them to his friends. Angela has "gotten" Jordan Catalano in some way, but it's not the way she's been yearning for.

Cut to English class. Jordan is in class but Angela isn't. English teacher Mr. Katimski walks up and down the aisles and reads Shakespeare's Sonnet 130, another Dark Lady sonnet, and one of Shakespeare's most well-known, aloud to his students:

> My mistress' eyes are nothing like the sun;
> Coral is far more red than her lips' red;
> If snow be white, why then her breasts are dun;
> If hairs be wires, black wires grow on her head;
> I have seen roses damasked, red and white,
> But no such roses see I in her cheeks;
> And in some perfumes is there more delight
> Than in the breath that from my mistress reeks.
> I love to hear her speak, yet well I know
> That music hath a far more pleasing sound;
> I grant I never saw a goddess go;
> My mistress, when she walks, treads on the
>   ground.
> And yet, by heaven, I think my love as rare
> As any she belied with false compare.

As Mr. Katimski reads, the camera makes its way to Jordan, who is unusually focused. His blue eyes are huge. At the couplet—which is also the volta—we see a look of recognition on his face. Jordan is not a good student. There is an episode of *My So-Called*

Life titled "Jordan Can't Read." But in this moment, Shakespeare's sonnet speaks to him as nothing ever has in literature class before. He is engaged, alert, and wide-eyed.

After he finishes reading the poem, Mr. Katimski asks the class: "What kind of girl is Shakespeare describing here? Is she, is she the most beautiful girl?" Angela's neighbor Brian Krakow answers first:

BRIAN: No.
MR. KATIMSKI: Is she a goddess? Physically perfect? The kind of girl who, um, stops traffic? When she walks down the street?
BRIAN: No.
MR. KATIMSKI: So he's not in love with her?
JORDAN: Yeah, he is.

Mr. Katimski looks at Jordan expectantly, and gestures his hands toward him, trying to pull answers from his shy student, until Brian eventually breaks in.

MR. KATIMSKI: Well, why is that? Why is he in love with her? What is it? What is it about her?
BRIAN: She's not just a fantasy. She's got, like, flaws. She's real.
MR. KATIMSKI: Thank you.

Mr. Katimski looks back at Jordan. Jordan smiles to himself. The camera hugs his beautiful face. We understand that he has gotten the poem. And at the end of the episode, Jordan acts on his revelation; he very publicly takes Angela's hand in the school hallway and asks her to talk. The sonnet has done its work.

When I first watched *My So-Called Life*, Angela was my avatar. How could she not be? But watching the show now, I also see myself in Mr. Katimski. I know what it feels like to read Shakespeare's Sonnet 130 to a room of young people who think that Shakespeare is boring and irrelevant. I have often taught this particular sonnet to classrooms of poetry novices because, unlike Sonnet 141, it is a poem that does not require a lot of unpacking for basic comprehension. Sonnet 130's syntax is unusually easy to understand. It is a sonnet for beginners.

Sonnet 130 lists all of the things the speaker does not like about the Dark Lady, and once you get that's what he's doing, you get it. This particular litany is a blazon, or a poetic trope in which the speaker catalogues all of the wonderful things about the body of his beloved through metaphor or simile. A traditional blazon claims: your eyes are like the sun! Your lips are like rubies! Your cheeks are like roses! Shakespeare, however, turns the blazon tradition inside out. Instead of praising all the parts of his beloved's body, he criticizes them. But at the volta at line 13, he changes his act: "And yet, by heaven, I think my love as rare / As any she belied with false compare." He thinks all of the other poets are being silly with their false, hyperbolic metaphors about their beloveds. The Dark Lady is as "rare" as any of the rest of the women whose beauty has been exaggerated by other sonneteers.

What Brian and Jordan take from the poem is that the mistress—the Dark Lady—is not "perfect." She may not stop traffic, but he loves her anyway. When I teach this poem, we talk about the many ways we might read it. We always start with a reading like Brian's. We end, though, with a closer look at the final lines. We think about what the sonnet has to say about poetry itself, about the work of metaphor and the sonneteers who have come before. The poem contemplates loving an imperfect woman, but it also pokes fun at the silliness of other writers and their over-the-top metaphors.

Jordan doesn't get to the second, more nuanced reading of the poem. The couplet is simply the occasion for him to realize his love for Angela. The poem's volta, at which point Jordan has his moment of recognition, is quite similar to the volta of Kat's poem in *10 Things I Hate about You*. Both of these poems stage for the characters a realization of love.

But it is also important, I think, that Kat's rewriting of Sonnet 141 replaces the sadomasochism of the poem with a simpler understanding of love, while Jordan's understanding of Sonnet 130 ignores the complexities of the final couplet and stops short of thinking about poetry as a form with traditions that can be transposed to powerful ends. Pop culture interpretations of Shakespeare omit nuances, which is just fine with me. Being a teenager is about big feelings and swift reversals and major realizations on the regular. In poetry terms, teenagehood is a volta. Who has the capacity for nuance at sixteen when every day you change, and every day life changes you?

In watching *My So-Called Life* for the first time in twenty years, I am touched not so much by Jordan's realization, but by Mr. Katimski's perception of it. There is a sense you develop as a poetry teacher—probably any kind of teacher but I experience it in the poetry classroom—a sense of that moment when some poem that is difficult and irrelevant and obscure suddenly becomes not at all so. When you look at a student and you can see them thinking, oh shit this poem is speaking to me. Or sometimes, oh *this is me*, or even better, *this could be me.* And then they walk out of your classroom and grab Angela's hand in front of everybody and you get to see that too.

* * *

I was in eighth grade when I first saw *William Shakespeare's Romeo + Juliet* (1996) at the multiplex. The film, which was directed by Baz Luhrmann, ignited a brief but intense obsession with Shakespeare and a much longer obsession with Leonardo DiCaprio. I memorized chunks of the play for fun; I bought a poster of Leo as Romeo at the mall; I yearned for someone to yearn for me at my window.

In graduate school, I would learn that the play is steeped in sonnets and sonnet culture, but I didn't know any of that at thirteen. What I did know:

Romeo and Juliet's eyes first meet across a huge fish tank at the Capulets' costume party. Des'ree is singing "I'm Kissing You," the most beautiful love song in the world. Their first ever conversation takes the form of a sonnet:

ROMEO
If I profane with my unworthiest hand
This holy shrine, the gentle sin is this:
My lips, two blushing pilgrims, ready stand
To smooth that rough touch with a tender kiss.

JULIET
Good pilgrim, you do wrong your hand too much,
Which mannerly devotion shows in this;
For saints have hands that pilgrims' hands do touch,
And palm to palm is holy palmers' kiss.

ROMEO
Have not saints lips, and holy palmers too?

JULIET
Ay, pilgrim, lips that they must use in prayer.

ROMEO
O, then, dear saint, let lips do what hands do;
They pray—grant thou, lest faith turn to despair.

JULIET
Saints do not move, though grant for prayers' sake.

ROMEO
Then move not, while my prayer's effect I take.

I am quite sure that when I first saw the film, I had no idea what Romeo and Juliet were saying to each other. I am sure I knew some things though: that they were flirting about kissing, that they were rhyming with each other, that they were at each other's level, that it was sweet and it was sexy, and that it ended with a makeout in an elevator.

Unlike the other sonnets in this chapter, this sonnet is not unidirectional. Romeo and Juliet create it together. What matters is the reciprocity. And I understood exactly what I needed to understand about it when I was thirteen: that two very attractive teens are bantering, punning, and flirting with each other in a manner so reciprocal that they manage to create a poem. The sonnet doesn't even have a volta, just the collaborative back-and-forth building toward a kiss, in which Romeo's fourteenth line rhymes with Juliet's thirteenth line, a kiss in a poem that leads to an actual kiss which leads to a full-on makeout session in a golden elevator, Romeo dressed as a knight, Juliet as an angel while "I'm Kissing You" plays again, this time as an orchestral version. It was wanting that was smart and so beautiful. It was everything that I wanted wanting to be. In between elevator kisses, Romeo whispers words I know I understood at thirteen: "O trespass sweetly urged, / Give me my sin again." The poem doesn't need a volta because the poem itself is a volta, a turning of plot that leaves a thirteen-year-old girl sobbing in her bed for hours after she has returned home from the multiplex. I knew nothing about the ravages of having in my own life, but oh the things I could learn from poems in the movies.

What I want to do by aligning these three sonnet moments in US pop cultural history is to show that the 1990s Shakespearean sonnet is not just about realizing and declaring desire, which is something it has been for a long time. These moments folded the sonnet into dramatic action to create the occasion for reciprocity. The sonnet says *I love you*, and creates the space for an *I love you too*. Patrick apologizing and meeting Kat where she was, Jordan grabbing Angela's hand and meeting her where she was, Romeo and Juliet realizing that they are meant to be—or at least at this point, meant to be making out—together. We learn in *Romeo + Juliet* that a sonnet is something that you might make together; in *10 Things I Hate about You* and *My So-Called Life*, we learn that a sonnet is something that might make you together. Popular media told white teen girls memorizing sonnets in seventh grade that a poem could be the start of something, the start of you getting what you wanted. It worked for Julia Stiles and it worked for Claire Danes, and maybe, please, poetry could bring a boy to me?

* * *

The only thing more embarrassing than one's own heterosexuality is one's own youthful heterosexuality. But I think that, all in all, identifying with alt-girls in teen media and an obsession with a cute professor's hair were not the worst way to get into poems, even if they gave me a pretty limited vision of what poems could be or could be for. In the first poem of his book *American Sonnets for My Past and Future Assassin*, a book of political sonnets about the United States published in 2018 in the middle of the Trump administration, contemporary Black poet Terrance Hayes also expresses some ambivalence about the way he got into poetry:

> The black poet would love to tell you his century began
> With Hughes or, God forbid, Wheatley, but actually
> It began with all the poetry weirdos & worriers, warriors,
> Poetry whiners & winos

And, I mean, same. Hayes is a good decade older than I am so I doubt his entrée to poetry involved Julia Stiles's blue camo tank top, but what we share, or at least what the speaker of this poem and I share, is an identification with and desire to be one of those "poetry weirdos." We all have our origin stories, even if they aren't what we wish they might be.

And how we got into poems isn't always an indication of where we end up in poems. Despite not getting into poetry by way of the Black American poetic tradition that includes poets like Phillis Wheatley and Langston Hughes, Hayes's *American Sonnets for My Past and Future Assassin* is a book very much steeped in that tradition. It is a book that, like Claude McKay's *Harlem Shadows* (1922), uses the sonnet to express the entwined forms of loving and hating that Shakespeare and Kat are so into. But in Hayes's hands, that ambivalence is transformed into being wanted and hated *by* a nation, while in McKay's, it is transformed into wanting and hating *of* a nation. McKay's and Hayes's sonnets are structured by the same sorts of feelings as Shakespeare's, but they are not about a singular love object; they are about a country and a people.

All of the poems in Hayes's book have the same title printed across the top of the page—"American Sonnet for My Past and Future Assassin"—in a repetition that insists on America's violent past and presumed violent future for Black Americans. The seventh poem begins:

> I lock you in an American sonnet that is part prison,
> Part panic closet, a little room in a house set aflame.
> I lock you in a form that is part music box, part meat
> Grinder to separate the song of the bird from the bone.
> I lock your persona in a dream-inducing sleeper hold
> While your better selves watch from the bleachers.
> I make you both gym & crow here.

This poem brings together complex metaphors of captivity and flight. The term "American sonnet" was coined by Black American poet Wanda Coleman in a 1994 book, and for Hughes, the American sonnet is a confined space: "part prison, / Part panic closet." The speaker of the poem is a generalized white American public aiming to confine its "you"—a figure of Hayes himself—into its forms of poetry and society. By punning on the name of Jim Crow laws, Hayes transforms American history through wordplay. He figures the nation as a "gym" (as in gymnasium) and the "you" as a "crow." Hayes went to college on an athletic scholarship and was an All-American basketball player. I suspect that this punning is quite personal.

The poem continues:

> . . . As the crow
> You undergo a beautiful catharsis trapped one
>   night
> In the shadows of the gym. As the gym, the feel
>   of crow-
> Shit dropping to your floors is not unlike the
>   stars
> Falling from the pep rally posters on your walls.
> I make you a box of darkness with a bird in its
>   heart.
> Voltas of acoustics, instinct & metaphor. It is not
>   enough
> To love you. It is not enough to want you
>   destroyed.

The figure of the crow, a figure Hayes uses throughout the book, might offer escape, but escape turns out to be impossible, because the speaker of the poem has trapped him in its "box of darkness." Within this American sonnet that is "a little room in a house"—a nation—"set aflame," "it is not enough / To love you. Is it not enough to want you destroyed." Hayes channels the voice of white America's ambivalent feelings toward Black Americans that it has literally and figuratively locked up in prisons, in panic closets, in little rooms, in the sonnet, where "voltas of acoustics, instinct & metaphor" converge as in an echoing gymnasium. The American sonnet—a stand-in for the US—is a place for white America to keep the "you" trapped, a Black "you" that it loves (for example, on the basketball court) and wants to destroy (for example, at the ballot box) while also tempting "you" with a vision of freedom. The sonnet recursively folds in on itself with its extended metaphors, like echoes in a large gymnasium, and it has no volta. It ends ambivalently while gesturing toward a violent future: what is ominously waiting outside the bounds of the sonnet for Black Americans if neither hate nor love is enough?

The ambivalence of white America's hate and love for African Americans that we see in Hayes's poem is a mirror image of the loving and hating in Claude McKay's poem "America" from almost ninety years before. McKay, who was born and raised in Jamaica and moved to the United States in 1912, wrote about his ambivalence toward the nation in his poem "America":

> Although she feeds me bread of bitterness,
> And sinks into my throat her tiger's tooth,
> Stealing my breath of life, I will confess
> I love this cultured hell that tests my youth.
> Her vigor flows like tides into my blood,
> Giving me strength erect against her hate,
> Her bigness sweeps my being like a flood.
> Yet, as a rebel fronts a king in state,
> I stand within her walls with not a shred
> Of terror, malice, not a word of jeer.
> Darkly I gaze into the days ahead,
> And see her might and granite wonders there,
> Beneath the touch of Time's unerring hand,
> Like priceless treasures sinking in the sand.

McKay's poem describes his speaker's relationship to and ambivalence about America from his opening lines onward. America may "sink into [his] throat her tiger's tooth," but he must "confess" that he loves her anyway. What the speaker finds sustaining about America is also what tortures him; America "flows like tides into [his] blood, / Giving [him] strength erect against her hate." Here we see a version of the ravages of having that we saw in Shakespeare's sonnets. Though McKay's main concern is political, he draws on Shakespeare's eroticized language to show how intimately he experiences those politics. The volta of the poem (at the "yet" of the eighth line) shifts from an explanation of the speaker's relationship to America to a premonition, a vision held by the outsider within the nation. McKay's speaker "darkly" "gaze[s] into the days ahead," when America's "might and granite wonders" will metaphorically sink into the sand. In this moment, I read these final lines of "America" and think of the insurrection at the US Capitol on January 6, 2021, and the white supremacist multitudes enveloping the building, the nation's racist history and present converging in an attempt to defy an election. Time's unerring hand, indeed.

* * *

It may seem silly to think about political sonnets by Hayes and McKay alongside Shakespeare's sonnets as they were animated and transformed in 1990s teen media, but what making these alignments reveals is how much of my youth was catered to people like me, which is to say, the suburban straight white girls of America. *10 Things I Hate about You*, *My So-Called Life*, and *Romeo + Juliet* allowed me to see poetry as a place for someone like me, a younger me who often felt like a bit of an outsider, a bit of a yearner, a bit of a "poetry weirdo" before I even was one. My media landscape was designed to make me feel affirmed in my sense of outsiderness, and to not show me anything at all of what actual political marginality— the kind we see in poems by Black poets such as

Hayes and McKay—looked like in the United States. "Poetry weirdo" is not a protected class.

When I was young, poetry felt like an opportunity. I was taught in school and on my screens that poetry was a space where I could figure out who I wanted to be and how to get what I wanted. And in some ways, it was, though I feel obligated to say that the sonnets I wrote in college convinced absolutely no one to be in love with me. (And believe me, I tried.) What now seems clear to me is that the opportunities that I saw in poetry were the opportunities I also saw open to me more generally, as a young white woman in the US at the beginning of a new millennium. So many things felt possible, because the sonnet for me never was part prison. It was not a little room in a house set aflame. No one was trying to separate my song from my bone. No one was trying to steal my breath of life in America. Even my outsiderness found a home on the main stage. These were the circumstances that brought me to poetry. I was so lucky, and I had no idea.

2

THE ALPHABET POEM

To Learn

My favorite alphabet book is Edward Gorey's deliciously morbid *The Gashlycrumb Tinies*. First published in 1963, the book tells the tales of twenty-six children—one for each letter of the alphabet—who suffer terrible deaths. It begins "A is for Amy who fell down the stairs" and continues: "B is for Basil assaulted by bears / C is for Clara who wasted away / D is for Desmond thrown out of a sleigh." Each child (and letter of the alphabet) gets their own page, which is illustrated in Gorey's signature Edwardian-esque crosshatched illustrations. The lines of the poem are precise rhyming couplets written in dactyls (a stressed syllable followed by two unstressed syllables) that give the poem a loping, falling feeling. Reading the book aloud feels not unlike tumbling down a steep, jagged hill. The book is a creepy good time, if you like that sort of thing, and I do.

In the book, Gorey sometimes illustrates children as already dead (as in Kate, who lays flat on the ground after being struck by an axe), but he more often draws them in the moments before their deaths. Prue is "trampled flat in a brawl," and we see her about to open a door to a crowded pub; Victor is "squashed under a train," and we see him standing on train tracks in silhouette, anticipating the train's arrival. My favorite page (because part of the fun of this book is having a favorite page) has always been "N is for Neville who died of ennui," which features a drawing of a large, cavernous window with the top half of a tiny child's face peeking out of it. If you were trapped alone in this bleakness, you might die of ennui too. The COVID-19 pandemic has given me a new perspective on how this might be true.

One of the many delights of *The Gashlycrumb Tinies* is that it takes a didactic children's form—the alphabet poem—and fills it with macabre words and images that you might not expect to find in a children's book. But this raises the question: is this a book that you want to read to your small child? Who is *The Gashlycrumb Tinies* really for? Toddlers learning the letters of the alphabet? Eight- or nine-year-olds who enjoy the original Grimms' fairy tales and other ghoulish children's stories? Parents seeking some amusement as they read their child to sleep? Alphabet poems and books always raise a question of audience, because if you already know the letters of the alphabet (and presumably this is the case if you are reading an alphabet poem on the page), you don't need the alphabet poem to teach you what it is, superficially at least, intended to teach.

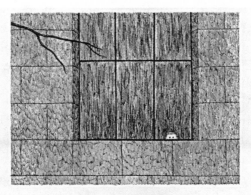

N is for NEVILLE who died of ennui

"N is for Neville who died of Ennui" from *The Gashlycrumb Tinies*, by Edward Gorey. © The Edward Gorey Charitable Trust

While some alphabet books—think children's classics like *Dr. Seuss's ABC* or *Chicka Chicka Boom Boom*—have a clear intent to teach new readers the letters of the alphabet, other alphabet books and poems address more ambiguous audiences. And even when an alphabet book addresses a toddler, its audience is always doubled; an already-literate person must by necessity be riding along, reading an alphabet book to a preliterate child. An author, then, might use the didactic form of the alphabet poem to smuggle in different lessons altogether, lessons that have nothing to do with the letters of the alphabet— lessons, even, that the author themselves might not perceive themselves as teaching. I always wonder if *The Gashlycrumb Tinies* actually does have a number of tiny lessons to impart—don't enter a brawl, don't stand by the train tracks, don't stay alone in a big empty house or you'll die of ennui—or if the major lesson is something more simple, like: childhood is just plain terrifying.

Alphabet poems introduce many of us to the genre of poetry; they are poems that we read or have read to us along with nursery rhymes and *Goodnight Moon* when we are still quite young and probably not yet aware of "poetry" as a category of anything. They are books read in and by small communities of readers, with parents, in play groups, at preschool. When I have taught introductory literature classes, I have sometimes dedicated a day to reading poetry for children, if for no other reason than to show students that poems aren't totally separated from their life experiences, that the first poem they encountered was not, in fact, Shakespeare's Sonnet 130, that they already know so many poems by heart there's no reason to be intimidated.

We read alphabet poems to children so that they can learn the letters of the alphabet, but if we've already learned our ABCs, why do we keep reading them? And why do poets keep writing them for readers who very well know their ABCs? Why does the form leap from childhood to adulthood? And what changes when it does? One of the things that intrigues me about these poems is the metaphorical weight the simple structure always carries. Not only is the Roman alphabet the foundation of written language in English, the sequence itself is a powerful tool for organizing. We sit in alphabetical order in grade school classrooms and we graduate in alphabetical order from high schools, colleges, and universities. Our personnel files are organized alphabetically, in filing cabinets and on computer screens. When we vote in the US, we check in with volunteers at the polls who locate us in electoral rolls of alphabetically ordered citizens. The alphabet organizes America.

Though the alphabetic sequence carries all of this cultural baggage, we organize things alphabetically precisely when we *don't* want to create meaning out of our orders. That's because the letters of the alphabet are arbitrary signifiers with no inherent meaning. A doesn't mean anything, and neither does B, and neither does C. E isn't worth more than D; it's just further along in the sequence. Writers of alphabet poems know that the alphabet can be a powerful tool of ordering the world and also a structure devoid of meaning. As a form, the alphabet poem brings together both the potential violence of ordering and the possibility of undermining violent orders via play with arbitrary signifiers. But alphabet poems also reveal how ordering—for those who are in control, who are doing the ordering—can be comforting, a way of fitting the status quo into a familiar form, a routinized way of moving through the world and shaping it according to a set of rules that have already been provided and that do not need to be scrutinized. Alphabetizing is easy. Combine all this with the alphabet's long association with children and didacticism, and you have a recipe for some very interesting poems that arrange, organize, and sometimes dismantle worlds for children (and adults) who are ready—or not—to learn.

* * *

When I was in graduate school, I wrote my dissertation on the alphabetic sequence in the experimental literature and visual art of the twentieth and twenty-first centuries. It was kind of an unusual topic then and now; it's not like I was entering a burgeoning field of alphabet studies. It was not on trend. (I have never been on trend.) But the fun thing about the topic is that whomever I shared it with always had an alphabet text to recommend to me: a favorite alphabet poem from childhood, an obscure book of avant-garde poetry, an experimental film from the 1980s, a sketch with a celebrity from *Sesame Street*, a billboard, a birthday card. Everyone—not just other academics in literature—wanted to talk about the alphabet with me. The alphabet feels like a form of life, not just a form of poetry. And when you embark on a years-long journey writing about the alphabet, you begin to see how much of American life is ordered from A to Z.

Alphabet poems have been around for a very long time. Longer than sonnets. And what I call an "alphabet poem" has gone by a number of different names—"abecedarian," "abecedarius," "abecedary," "abecedarium"—over thousands of years. Psalm 119 in the Bible, for example, consists of twenty-two stanzas, one for each letter of the Hebrew alphabet. In Chaucer's Middle English poem "ABC" from the fourteenth century, the first letter of each stanza proceeds alphabetically; the first word of the first stanza is "Almighty," the first word of the second stanza is "Bountee," and so on. Other alphabet poems restrict their writers aggressively. Robert Pinsky's poem "ABC," for example, is a twenty-six-word poem in which each word begins with the subsequent letter of the alphabet. The first line reads: "Any body can die, evidently." (Poets, they do love writing about death.) While all (or most) alphabet poems begin with A and end with Z, the way that they move from A to Z can vary infinitely. As a poet, you can get creative with the form and still have it be extremely recognizable as an alphabet poem. In this way, alphabet poems are very unlike sonnets, which in their fourteen lines are fairly rigid as forms of poetry. An alphabet poem can have 26 words, or 26 lines, or 260 lines and still be considered an alphabet poem.

Alphabet poems appear everywhere in post-1945 American poetry. If you look hard enough (and I have), chances are you'll find an alphabet poem or two within your favorite poet's oeuvre. A number of poets have even written book-length collections of poetry engaged with the alphabetic sequence as a form. In 2001, when I was writing my first bad sonnets in college, Harryette Mullen published *Sleeping with the*

Dictionary, an entire book that she organized alphabetically, as a glimpse at the table of contents reveals. The collection features at least one poem for every letter of the alphabet except for I, U, and Y. Her poem "Why You and I," which begins "Who knows why you and I fell off the roster?" acknowledges and questions these omissions, while also playing with the fact that these letters are homophones. This is signature Mullen: alphabet play, word games, and a dash of social critique. As a Black experimental poet—one of the few from her generation of Language poets who have been canonized—the question of inclusion, of "who knows why you and I fell off" (or were included) "on the roster" (in the first place) is more than just a joke about homophones for Mullen. She continues with more, similar questions: "Who can figure why you and I never passed muster / on our way out yonder" and "Could anyone guess, does anyone know or even care / why you and I can't be found, as hard as we look?" The questions of inclusion and exclusion—of who gets to count in our ordering structures—are serious topics for poets who have traditionally been excluded from poetry communities and the scholarly histories we tell about them.

For hundreds of years, the most widely read alphabet poem in the United States could be found in the *New England Primer*. The *Primer* was first published in the American colonies in the late seventeenth century, and it was reprinted (often with variations) and used to instruct millions of children

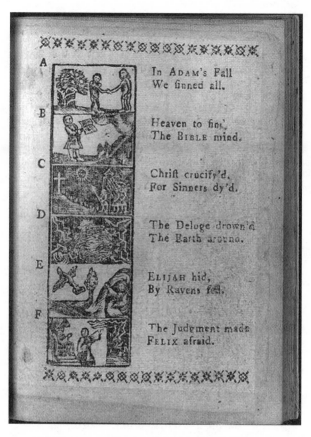

A — In ADAM's Fall
We sinned all.

B — Heaven to find,
The BIBLE mind.

C — Christ crucify'd,
For Sinners dy'd.

D — The Deluge drown'd
The Earth around.

E — ELIJAH hid,
By Ravens fed.

F — The Judgment made
FELIX afraid.

Page from *The New England Primer Improved*, letters A through F, illus., 1773. https://www.loc.gov/item/2006683472/

in homes and school rooms across the country up through the early twentieth century. You cannot overstate its ubiquity. It was about ninety pages long and included a mix of all kinds of didactic materials. In addition to its alphabet poem, it included prayers, alphabetized lists of syllables and words, catechisms, dialogues, and more. In the *New England Primer*, language instruction, Puritan religious instruction, and community making go hand in hand.

While the text of the alphabet poem of the *Primer* varies among editions, the basic structure remains the same. Moving from the left to right side of the page, we see the printed letter of the alphabet itself, followed by an image, and then followed by a terse rhyming couplet. In a 1773 edition of the *Primer*, the first image features Eve giving Adam the forbidden fruit, while the serpent looks on. The poem begins with a bang: "In Adam's Fall / We sinned all." What a way to introduce the letters of the alphabet to a small child! The *Primer* creates a world that inculcates new readers into the alphabet, and written language more generally, alongside knowledge of the fall of man. "All" of us are included in Adam's fall. This is a pretty grim way to begin learning the alphabet and make a community of new readers.

But fear not, new readers, because language can also save. The next couplet tells us "Heaven to find / The Bible mind." The image features a small child holding open a book, presumably the Bible, heaven-ward. We may all sin, but the Bible may redeem us and provide the way to Heaven. Note that the *New England Primer* doesn't announce "A is for Adam" or "B is for the Bible"; the letters themselves are woven into the lines of the poem. The religious lessons take precedence over the alphabetic instruction, as the world is sorted not just alphabetically, but by who is saved and who is not.

The poem continues with more religious instruction: "Christ crucify'd / For sinners dy'd. / The Deluge drown'd / The Earth around." Is all this death and destruction starting to feel familiar? The experience of reading the *Primer* feels like the experience of reading *The Gashlycrumb Tinies*, except pious rather than goth. Every other couplet reveals another violent story from the Bible: the fall of man, the crucifixion of Christ, the flood, and so on. Not all versions of the poem are so Christianity-heavy, but most are just as morbid. When I first researched the *Primer*, I went actively looking for a kinder, friendlier edition that was perhaps less macabre. I found one, in which C was not for "Christ crucify'd," but for "Cat." You can imagine my reaction, then, when I looked at the image of a cat playing with a mouse and then read the full couplet: "The Cat doth play / and after slay." Edward Gorey wrote neither the first nor the last alphabet poem that matches violent content with sing-songy rhymes. As we will continue to see, alphabetical ordering itself can be a form of violence.

* * *

In one of my graduate school classes, I read a series of alphabet poems in the book *Modern Life* by poet Matthea Harvey, and I found them intriguing and strange, and I got that itch about them, that sense that I could do something with them, that I might want to write about them some day. The sequences were titled "The Future of Terror" and "Terror of the Future." It was clear that they were very much about the moment's politics, but I didn't feel equipped to write about them at the time. The Global War on Terror had been waging for six years. It was all so big.

Later, while I was reading a ton of books for my comprehensive exams and casting about for big dissertation ideas, I stopped at a second-hand furniture store on the way home from campus. I walked into a small room of used books and it was there that I found a slim and tall pink book titled *The Gertrude Stein First Reader and Three Plays*. I spent some time flipping through it and realized it was a children's book. Imagine that: an experimental writer known for pushing the boundaries of language writing in a children's form. How strange! I got that fluttery, sweaty feeling that promptly arrives with a new crush or a new idea. (Of course, a new idea is also a new crush.)

I bought the book, drove home, did some googling, and found out that Gertrude Stein had written several books for children. One of them was titled *To Do: A Book of Alphabets and Birthdays*. I ordered used copies of all of her children's books. I wrote down their library call numbers because I couldn't actually wait for my copies to arrive. I did some quick research and realized that they had barely been written about by anyone. *To Do: A Book of Alphabets and Birthdays* had been published only after Stein's death and been basically ignored by scholars. I had stumbled upon a very minor book by a very major author of the kind of experimental literature that I was into, and the alphabet organized it. That fluttery feeling returned; Stein's alphabet book could be my ticket to something. I promptly immersed myself in alphabet poems and books, attempting to get to know the lay of the alphabet land.

As I collected alphabet poems and books, I came across a number of them from the nineteenth-century United States. They were not within the scope of my dissertation but they very much influenced how I thought about the alphabet as a form, and they helped me answer the questions that I was interested in asking throughout my dissertation: why do poets use the alphabetic sequence, when it is a form so associated with children and childishness, if they are not trying to teach the alphabet? Who do alphabet books imagine they are for? What does the alphabet mean for the work poetry can do in the world?

The *Anti-Slavery Alphabet* (1846) and *A Coon Alphabet* (1898), both nineteenth-century texts presumably addressed to children, use the alphabetic sequence to reentrench racist ideologies of their time. While it was published anonymously, most attribute the *Anti-Slavery Alphabet* to Quaker sisters Hannah and Mary Townsend. The sisters distributed it at the Philadelphia Anti-Slavery Fair, an annual event sponsored by the Philadelphia Female Anti-Slavery Society. The book begins with a direct address, "To Our Little Readers":

> Listen, little children, all,
> Listen to our earnest call:
> You are very young, 'tis true,
> But there's much that you can do.
> Even you can plead with men
> That they buy not slaves again,
> And that those they have may be
> Quickly set at liberty.

The poem continues in the form of an "alphabet array," a term coined by Patricia Crain in her book about the alphabet, in which we see the same "A is for" "B is for" as in *The Gashlycrumb Tinies*:

> A is an Abolitionist—
> A man who wants to free
> The wretched slave—and give to all
> An equal liberty.
>
> B is a Brother with a skin
> Of somewhat darker hue,
> But in our Heavenly Father's sight,
> He is as dear as you.

The poem believes that it is speaking to "children all," but, when we read closely, we find that it speaks to a very limited version of "all." The *Anti-Slavery Alphabet* explicitly figures the "we" as a *white* we. The "Abolitionist"—"A man who wants to free / The wretched slave"—is, in this poem, male and white. Grammatically, he is the subject, able to do things, perform actions, while the "wretched slave" is the object who can do nothing. And in the next stanza, B is for the Black "Brother" with "a skin of / Somewhat darker hue" who is "as dear as you." That tiny "you" is everything. It assumes that "you"—the reader— are not Black. By omitting Black readers from its audience, the poem—which frequently addresses its readers directly—shows its racist understanding of the project of abolition. In this poem, abolition is something that white people do for Black people, not something that Black people might do for themselves or each other. The poem can't imagine enslaved people as human beings with subjectivities or agency or even lives of their own. The *Anti-Slavery Alphabet* teaches white children to become white saviors.

The poem prints each quatrain next to a large, decorative graphic of its corresponding letter, and each letter of the alphabet stands for something in the antebellum US related to slavery or abolition. Like many abolitionist texts from the nineteenth century, it deploys the pain of Black people for political purposes, and ultimately reinforces the violence that it purportedly seeks to end. As we read past "A" and "B" in the poem, we see that it reproduces the widespread practices, symbols, and tropes of American slavery. "C" is for "Cotton-field," "F" is for "Fugitive," "K" is for "Kidnapper," and "W" is for "Whipping post." The white authors have created an alphabet array of torture:

> W is the Whipping post,
> > To which the slave is bound,
> While on his naked back, the lash
> > Makes many a bleeding wound.

The poem is gratuitous in its representation of violence. And the horror of the content—the image of an enslaved person tied to a whipping post—sits cruelly next to the sing-songy rhymes and childish alphabet form. This stanza also omits the enslaver from the scene of brutality; the poem represents the whip as acting of its own accord. It is the whip doing the whipping, not the white enslaver.

If the *Anti-Slavery Alphabet*'s racism works implicitly, then E. W. Kemble's *A Coon Alphabet*, as its title suggests, offers its racism explicitly. The scholar Elvin Holt has called it a "primer of racial prejudice." *A Coon Alphabet*, like the *Anti-Slavery Alphabet*, is an alphabet array. Its twenty-six quatrains, written in a crude parody of Black dialect, unfold with detailed drawings over two pages, each representing an act of violence perpetrated against the bodies of Black people, mostly children. The children in the book conform to stereotypes that have circulated in the US for hundreds of years; they have bulging eyes, exaggerated lips, messy hair. The book falls very much within the tradition of minstrelsy.

The violence of Kemble's book is not always explicit within the language of the poem, but it is always visible in its drawings. The book's first quatrain and image pairing depict a young Black child being thrown violently off his mule: "A is for Amos / what rides on ole mule / so he can be early / each monin ter school." The Black people in Kemble's book exist to be hurt; they suffer all kinds of pain, both accidentally and purposefully inflicted. Despite the differences in their stated politics, Kemble's book shares its attachment to Black pain with the *Anti-Slavery Alphabet*; both make suffering the logic of Black lives.

Like the *Anti-Slavery Alphabet*, Kemble's book announces its audience in its very first pages, before the alphabet poem even begins. The *Anti-Slavery Alphabet* begins with an address to an (implicitly) white "you." Kemble's book claims a Black one; in its frontispiece, a young Black girl sits with an ABC book open on her lap. This image suggests that this young girl is reading the very book that she is in. It doubles down on the "joke" of the book, that this minstrelized language and violent images are in fact how Black children learn. But it's unlikely that any

Black child in the United States needs an alphabet book to teach them the ABCs of racism. Kemble's real reader is a white one, here to be entertained by the show of suffering.

While we might like to think that the days of racist alphabet poems are of the past, these texts have a way of sticking around. *A Coon Alphabet* is available for purchase on Amazon and has a four-star rating on Goodreads. Alphabet books endure.

* * *

Nineteenth-century alphabet poems do damage, but they're not the only ones; seemingly banal political poems by white people do damage in the twenty-first century as well. One of the first contemporary poems that I found when I began working on my dissertation was Billy Collins's alphabet poem "The Names," which is a memorial for the victims of the September 11 terrorist attacks. (Maybe I should say now that I am not a fan of Collins, and especially not of this poem.) He wrote the poem in 2002 while I was still in college and he was the US poet laureate, and he read the poem aloud in a special joint session of Congress on the one-year anniversary of the attacks. "The Names" is not a strict alphabet poem in which each line or word begins with a successive letter of the alphabet. Instead, the poem is an elegy—a lament for the dead—in which the speaker of the poem encounters, via the alphabet, the victims of the terrorist attacks. The poem begins:

Yesterday, I lay awake in the palm of the night.
A soft rain stole in, unhelped by any breeze,
And when I saw the silver glaze on the windows,
I started with A, with Ackerman, as it happened,
Then Baxter and Calabro,
Davis and Eberling, names falling into place
As droplets fell through the dark.
Names printed on the ceiling of the night.
Names slipping around a watery bend.
Twenty-six willows on the banks of a stream.

The poem's investment in alphabetical order is not subtle; the speaker of the poem announces "I started with A," cuing readers into its alphabet schema immediately. But the poem acknowledges that there is an arbitrariness to this order. The speaker continues: "I started with A, with Ackerman, as it happened," and the phrase "as it happened" shows us that Ackerman is just one of many possible "A" names. The "Ackerman" is a synecdoche, in which one name stands for many. Within the familiar comforts of the alphabetic sequence, "names [fall] into place." There is no agency involved in this falling into place, Billy Collins would have us believe.

Collins memorializes the victims with a careful democracy. He alphabetizes the list of names as a way to avoid creating a hierarchy among them. "Ackerman" isn't somehow worth more or less than "Baxter"; A just comes before B in the alphabet. Collins's chosen names also suggest that the victims were a diverse group of Americans, which, in fact, they were. I'd bet a lot of money that Collins carefully chose these names to represent people of a number of racial and ethnic backgrounds. Lines such as "then Gonzalez and Han, Ishikawa and Jenkins," for example, ask us to remember that Latinx people, that Korean Americans and Japanese Americans, were killed in the attacks alongside white people.

"The Names," however, is curiously or—I think—not so curiously absent of Middle Eastern or South Asian names, though of course a number of people of Middle Eastern and South Asian descent died in the attacks. Names of Muslims, or those who *might* be read as Muslims by Collins's audience (in this case, both houses of Congress and Dick Cheney) do not have a place in "The Names." Like many other elegies, the poem has an impulse to collect and to contain and to approach tragedy through synecdoche—to let a part stand in for the whole of the grief. But the names of those who *might*—and I cannot stress this enough—*might* share their race, ethnicity, or religion with the perpetrators of the September 11 attacks have no place in Collins's poem. The absence of these names is jarring. I have taught this poem many times. My students, who have all grown up in the world that the War on Terror made, always notice the absences.

In his poem, Collins does what critic David Simpson suggests that many large-scale memorials of the attacks attempt to do: he insists on the value of the lives that were lost. In Simpson's words, memorialization renders victims "worthy of sacrifice" and suggests that their lives are "saturated with meaning." Through memorials of all kinds, victims become "heroes, sacrificial victims, icons of patriotic life." If we think of "The Names" in this context, we are left to ask ourselves: if Collins conspicuously omits the names of anyone who might be read as Muslim in his A to Z memorialization of the victims of 9/11, what value does he place on those lives? By purposefully omitting those with Middle Eastern or South Asian–seeming names from his carefully compiled alphabet, Collins claims that those particular victims of the attacks don't count.

To be a Muslim—or, more exactly, to have the possibility of being read by others as Muslim—locates one outside of the A to Z totality of the United States in Collins's poem. Victims with last names such as Chowdhury, Habib, and Shajahan (and there were victims with these last names) are not, by the logic of the poem, Americans. They are not existentially significant in this very significant poem that was read in front of a joint session of Congress on the first anniversary of the attacks. The alphabetic sequence, which makes its ethos of inclusion and exclusion quite visible, can be a powerful device of claiming who counts and who doesn't in US life.

It can also provide someone like Billy Collins a veneer of objectivity. I once gave a presentation at an academic conference in which I talked about this

poem and another participant in my seminar argued with me about my reading. Aren't you reading
too much into this, he asked. Wasn't Collins "just"
choosing names of victims randomly, and wasn't
that the whole point of alphabetizing the names in
the first place? Shouldn't we give him the benefit of
the doubt? I disagreed, and elaborated on my reading of the poem. He argued with me again. He used
the phrase "benefit of the doubt" again. I answered
again, unwavering, and he argued with me another
time. It was far from the first time that someone had
challenged my ideas, of course, but his vehemence
sticks with me. It was the vehemence of a white man
who feels implicated when you say: this shit is hateful, and we should talk about why and how it matters
and who it hurts.

* * *

As I was collecting all of these alphabet poems
and books—many of which led me down paths I'd
never expected—and as I watched my friends going
through their processes of choosing dissertation topics, I wondered what my alphabet project said about
me, but I didn't do much wondering aloud. In graduate school, I received the message that your personal
relationship to your work is the last thing you are
supposed to talk about. Your research is supposed
to be animated by your intellect and only your intellect, as if that could be separated from the rest of
you. And I don't think I would have (or even could

have) articulated this when I was working on my dissertation, but I think I ended up writing about the alphabet because of my cathection to school and learning. School is what I am good at. Intellectual engagement, more than almost anything else, makes me feel happy, engaged, alert, alive. School is where I have always felt I belonged.

Studying alphabet poems and texts, I think, was a way of engaging that feeling intellectually. I could spend time with poems and books and works of art that were interested in knowledge, in teaching and learning, that took education and learning and school as valid objects of study in and of themselves. I could think critically about texts that were trying—for better or for worse—to teach lessons. In Virginia Woolf's novel *To the Lighthouse*, Mr. Ramsay, the frustrated philosopher, imagines that all the knowledge in the world is arranged from A to Z. He gets stuck at the letter Q. Only one man in a generation, he thinks, can reach Z. Mr. Ramsay is a foolish figure in the novel; Woolf clearly doesn't endorse his alphabetic ways of thinking. But I have always understood Mr. Ramsay deeply. The alphabetic sequence promises order; it is a way of organizing and imposing meaning on a chaotic world. This way of thinking appeals to me.

But as we have seen, the forms of order that the alphabet imposes can be dangerous and cruel, and the alphabet poem often has a pernicious lesson to teach. What is a comforting and familiar form to some (ahem, Billy Collins) can be a form of violence in the way it imposes on and orders others. This, too, is something I learned anew in graduate school: the institutions that are supposed to protect us are often the ones that do us the most harm. As someone who has built a career in education, this is a lesson I learn again and again.

* * *

Solmaz Sharif's alphabet poem "Safe House" works very differently than the other alphabet poems we've seen so far. It appears in her 2016 poetry collection *Look*, which structures itself around a very particular alphabetized text: the US Department of Defense's *Dictionary of Military and Associated Terms.* Reading *Look*, you feel the presence of this dictionary palpably. Throughout the collection, Sharif prints the words that she has taken from the military dictionary in small caps so that they are starkly visible on the page. We can sense the military dictionary—a synecdoche for the US military itself—lurking behind every poem.

Sharif includes an important note about the *Dictionary of Military and Associated Terms* in *Look*. She tells us that she composed the book with the 2007 edition of the dictionary. Despite the fact that the Department of Defense updates its dictionary regularly, she continued to use this particular edition as she wrote. This is, of course, a practical decision. It seems like a lot of work to keep up with a regularly changing dictionary. But I also find this decision (and her announcement of it) telling, because it insists on Sharif's embodied writing practice. Sharif tells us: hey, there is a real human person behind these poems. I have written them and it has taken years of effort. That poems have authors who write them is not news, of course, but in the context of the topics of her poems—the Iran-Iraq war and the death of Sharif's uncle, Sharif's immigration to the US (she was born in Turkey to Iranian parents), the US wars in Iraq and Afghanistan, the brutality of US drone warfare—Sharif's insistence on her own agency becomes essential.

When reading *Look*, you can feel the surveillance of the US military embedded in every one of Sharif's poems. Each line of the poem "Safe House" begins with a different word from the *Dictionary of Military and Associated Terms* in alphabetical order. The poem starts with the word "sanctuary" and ends with the phrase "short fall." Sharif never gets outside S. When the poem opens, we are faced with a kind of lament for the "safe house" of the title that would offer sanctuary (and doesn't). Sharif begins by imagining what this safe house might look and feel like:

> SANCTUARY where we don't have to
> SANITIZE hands or words or knives, don't have
>   to use a
> SCALE each morning, worried we take up too
>   much space. I

SCAN my memory of baba talking on
SCREEN answering a question (*how are you?*) I
    would ask and ask from behind the camera,
    his face changing with each repetition as he
    tried to watch the football game. He doesn't
    know this is the beginning of my
SCRIBING life: repetition and change.

"Safe House" begins with a wish for safety and a moment of intimacy between father and daughter, the two of them talking to each other via small screens from across the world. But something feels forced in this poem; the whole thing feels constrained by the alphabetized words from the military dictionary at the beginning of each line. The military words create dramatic enjambments, or line breaks that come in the middle of sentences or clauses. They create a feeling of force behind the language, as if something else—alphabetical order, determined by the military dictionary—dictates the shape of her poem. Which it does.

As "Safe House" proceeds, intimacy and the threat of violence intertwine:

    . . . He kept our house
SECURE except from the little bugs that come
    with dried herbs from Iran. He gives
SECURITY officers a reason to get off their
    chairs. My father is not afraid of
SEDITION. He can

SEIZE a wild pigeon off a Santa Monica street or
    watch
SEIZURES unfold in his sister's bedroom—the
    FBI storming through. He said *use wood sticks*
    to hold up your protest signs then use them in
SELF-DEFENSE *when the horses come*

As we read these lines, a portrait emerges: the poem creates an image of the speaker's father, a brave provider. But it does so within the confines of the words from the DOD's *Dictionary of Military and Associated Terms.* The words from the dictionary act as a kind of embedded surveillance. They threaten the speaker's father, who himself is read as a threat (presumably because of his name, the color of his skin) to security officers. US military words have seeped into the domestic space and overtaken the poem. Here and in many of her poems, Sharif avoids a straightforward narrative—Why are the speaker and her father separated? Who is going to which protests?—but opaqueness works as part of Sharif's strategy. The alphabetized and arbitrarily ordered words from the military dictionary dominate the poem, just as US military interventions, invasions, and drone warfare have dominated the lives of the Iranian American members of Sharif's family.

In an interview, Sharif explains that her plans for *Look* changed as she began writing it. At first, she says, she "want[ed] to redefine the terms to reveal the truth beneath the terms." But then she tells us that the focus of the book changed. The poems "evolved into revealing those terms as a part of our lives everywhere, daily in the US." Instead of rewriting dictionary language, Sharif *reveals* how the military, with its dictionary's alphabetized language as well as its other weapons, structures and threatens everyday American life. In "The Names," Billy Collins's alphabet provides a veneer of objectivity. In "Safe House," Sharif pushes back against the form that so many white poets find comfort in. Collins conceals his accountability within his alphabetic form, while Sharif reveals the complicity of white Americans in the violence and destruction that the US has wrought within its borders and around the world.

* * *

It is perhaps needless to say that I did not end my dissertation where I started it. Which is good! If you knew where your research was going to lead you, there would be no reason to do it in the first place. Looking back from the vantage point of a few years, I think the most useful things that I learned from my project are these two ideas that I keep coming back to: first, that the lessons that alphabet poems think they're teaching are often not the ones that they are actually teaching, and second, that, for those doing the ordering, ordering can be a kind of comfort, a creation or restoration of familiar power structures. For those being ordered: well, ordering can be a form of violence. In this, *The Gashlycrumb Tinies* is not some kind of alphabetic outlier; the violence of ordering is baked into the form itself. And as we so often encounter alphabet poems within a didactic framework, alphabet poems reveal violence that's often bound to education.

This has been an invaluable lesson for me to learn as an educator. Researching alphabet poems and other didactic texts gave me a set of questions, questions that I carry with me as I teach and mentor and support college students: what do I think that I am teaching and what am I *actually* teaching? What are the gaps between what I am saying and how it is received by my students? What is my positionality to the material and to my students, and what does my body bring into every space it enters? What subtle lessons am I teaching through the works I assign, the way I organize a syllabus, how I write an email, how I share my space on a Zoom screen? When I am teaching poetry, who am I addressing, and who am I leaving out?

These questions are not just for those of us who work in education. As we have seen, the questions that alphabet poems ask—about ordering, address, inclusion, and exclusion—are important questions for the public sphere as well. In a country built and sustained by racial capitalism, in which we have been historically ordered by our racial, gender, and class identities in our homes and neighborhoods, in the census, by our employers and in our financial lives, the ordering and categorizing of people is always a political act. For hundreds of years, alphabet poems have been ordering American children and adults both through language instruction and the teaching of all kinds of other, more pernicious lessons, many about who does and doesn't belong. As Harryette Mullen asks in "Why You and I": "Who'll spell out for us, if we exist, / why you and I missed our turn on the list?"

3

THE DOCUMENTARY POEM

To Resist

In 2014, the poet and critic Cathy Park Hong published an exquisite essay describing the contemporary poetry scene and its history. The essay—"Delusions of Whiteness in the Avant-Garde"—accurately assesses the absence of writers of color from the scholarly histories of experimental poetry. In the essay, Hong, who would go on to publish the bestselling and award-winning book *Minor Feelings*, writes that "American avant-garde poetry has been an overwhelmingly white enterprise, ignoring major swaths of innovators—namely poets from past African American literary movements—whose prodigious writings have vitalized the margins, challenged institutions, and introduced radical languages and forms that avant-gardists have usurped without proper acknowledgment." This article brought to a wider (and whiter) audience a topic of conversation that many poets of color, especially those in and on the fringes of institutionally supported avant-garde and experimental poetry communities, had been having for years: that those communities were very white and often hostile to poets of color while also appropriating the very ideas and techniques of those poets.

In her essay, Hong identifies Kenneth Goldsmith, a contemporary white conceptual poet, as having a particular "delusion of whiteness." Hong borrows this term from James Baldwin, and she explains that white avant-garde poets from the early twentieth century onward have longed to be "post-identity," to write from some sort of neutral and objective subject position that simply does not exist. (This yearning for objectivity is, I will add, something we see in mainstream white poets, such as Billy Collins, as well.) Hong writes that "the avant-garde's 'delusion of whiteness' is the luxurious opinion that anyone can be 'post-identity' and can casually slip in and out of identities like a video game avatar, when there are those who are consistently harassed, surveilled, profiled, or deported for whom they are." Hong's critiques are both sociological (in terms of poetry community formation and canonization) and technical (in terms of poetic methods). For Hong, Goldsmith, both a poet and anthologist whose book publications reify communities and canons, is doubly problematic.

Hong's article proved to be all too acute when Kenneth Goldsmith made headlines the following year in 2015. At Interrupt 3, a language arts conference at Brown University, Goldsmith stood on a stage in front of an audience of seventy-five people and performed a poem titled "The Body of Michael Brown." For his performance, Goldsmith read aloud the autopsy report of the slain teenager, who was killed by a police officer the previous summer in Ferguson, Missouri, and whose death catalyzed the Black Lives Matter movement. Many at the event found the performance racist, and news of it spread quickly on social media, where it seemed that everyone found it racist.

The reason for this is that it *was* racist. In reading Michael Brown's autopsy aloud, Goldsmith spectacularized the death of a young Black man at the hands of the police for his poetic gain. And quite literally: he was paid a speaker's fee to read his poems at this event. It was an act of appropriation and exploitation, an intensified version of the theft Hong had already described. Michael Brown's death was not Goldsmith's story to tell, and if Goldsmith even considered the feelings a Black member of his audience might have— the suffering they might feel upon hearing the autopsy report of a Black victim of police brutality read at a poetry reading—he at best disregarded that suffering. Worse still is to imagine he *did* imagine those feelings, and invited them all the same. Nothing about the performance indicated that he considered his own positionality, his own implication in the structures of white supremacy. The performance itself was an iteration of the original act of police violence. Goldsmith was a white man profiting off of the aestheticization of Black suffering and death, and while he decided to donate his conference speaker fee to Michael Brown's family after the backlash, the harm he did with his performance was already done.

A few years previously, Goldsmith, the most well-known experimental poet of the early twenty-first century, had been invited to read his work at "An Evening of Poetry" at the Obama White House. He read selections of Walt Whitman's "Crossing Brooklyn Ferry" alongside poems from his own book *Traffic*, which consisted of transcribed New York radio traffic updates, often involving the Brooklyn Bridge. *Traffic* is an example of conceptual poetry, or "uncreative writing," in which the poet makes poetry out of already existing language and doesn't write anything new. In *Traffic* and "The Body of Michael Brown," Goldsmith imagines that he is presenting information neutrally; he situates himself as a conveyor of meaning created by others, rather than as a creator in and of himself. While many mainstream poets and critics didn't like what Goldsmith was doing, many white avant-garde poets and critics did. In the world of avant-garde poetics, of which I was a part, Goldsmith was a big deal.

Goldsmith's Interrupt 3 performance occurred in the latter half of the second Obama administration, in the swell of the Black Lives Matter movement, four months after the publication of Hong's "Delusions of Whiteness in the Avant-Garde," and seven months before Idusuyi would read Rankine's *Citizen* at a Trump rally. The performance became a catalyst for a very public conversation about poetry and whiteness, the likes of which I had never seen before outside of an academic setting. The year 2015 was a moment when many writers of color were speaking up—and not just speaking up but being heard by the white cultural establishment—about racism in cultural institutions, from the publishing industry to academia. Poets and collectives such as Mongrel Coalition against Gringpo responded to Goldsmith's performance forcefully as the story circulated on Twitter and was then picked up by more mainstream media. The Black feminist writer Roxane Gay tweeted, "the audacity of reading an autopsy report and calling it poetry," which pretty succinctly captures the mood of the internet. For Gay and others, Goldsmith's performance was doubly problematic: not only did he read Brown's autopsy report aloud, but he also had the "audacity" to call the autopsy report "poetry." I don't think that Gay is too concerned about the definition of poetry here, or that Goldsmith violated poetry's sacred status. Instead, she considers the limits of poetry. She criticizes how Goldsmith took a document of violence and aestheticized it, turned a record of suffering into "art." For Gay and the many other writers of color who responded to the performance, Goldsmith's conceptual methods were invested in these "delusions of whiteness," in which white poets believed that they could produce poetry out of already existing materials and present some kind of objective truth about them.

When mainstream outlets from the *New Yorker* to the *Huffington Post* to the *Guardian* picked up the story of Goldsmith's performance, I carefully watched the news cycle unfold. The Goldsmith situation felt close to me. I had written a dissertation chapter on Goldsmith and just published an article on him. This was a poet whose work—and whose self, which is very much a part of his work—I knew a lot about, and oh boy did I have things to say. I was never a cheerleader for Goldsmith, and my own academic work on his poetry was deeply skeptical of his frequent self-mythologizing, which seems to me to be very much based in his supposition of white male neutrality. I did, however, think that Goldsmith's poetry and methods were worth writing about and teaching, and I understood his work within the context of the avant-garde poetry movements that I had spent my graduate career studying. But thinking about the incident within the framework of Hong's "Delusions of Whiteness and the Avant-Garde" and learning from the many other poets who responded to Goldsmith's performance on social media and in print helped me see that his centrality to the contemporary conversations about poetry, the very conversations that I was involved in, was a problem in and of itself. I was a white woman reifying through my scholarly work the same structures of whiteness that Goldsmith was implicated in. What would happen if I moved Goldsmith from the center to the periphery in my understanding of the experimental poetry scene? How would my reading of the poetry of the twenty-first century change if I put experimental poets of color at the center?

As I reframed my understanding of my poetic moment through the lens of Hong and the many other critics who stepped up to critique Goldsmith, I saw that so many of the questions and techniques that Goldsmith and other conceptual poets were interested in had been employed long before them, that poets of color were using those techniques at the very same time as Goldsmith for very different purposes and receiving much less attention for them. And not just attention, but the material things that come with attention: publications, prizes, money, jobs teaching poetry, which is one of the few ways anyone can make a living in poetry these days. So many poets of the twenty-first century have, like Goldsmith, engaged directly with traumatic American pasts by incorporating all kinds of historical and legal documents in their poems. But unlike Goldsmith, these other poets—M. NourbeSe Philip, Layli Long Soldier, and J. Michael Martinez—have created documentary poems that expose the US's forms of oppression not to reinforce them, but to resist them. They do not reinflict horrors on an unsuspecting public, but instead ask questions about how to ethically represent and understand America's violent past and present. Documentary poems by these writers engage and counter official histories; for them, the aestheticizing potential power of poetry amplifies voices historic documents have too often silenced.

* * *

Documentary poems depend on different qualities than sonnets or alphabet poems. You can't identify them by counting lines or syllables, or by recognizing certain patterns or repetitions. Instead, documentary poems—which are usually long, and often book-length—want to represent the world as it is or was. They use empirical evidence—often in the form of quotes, reproduced historical and legal documents, and photographs—to make a political statement about a particular set of events. They incorporate the evidence directly into the poem, reproducing full or partial archival documents in the body of the text. And by using empirical evidence aesthetically, documentary poems incorporate, remake, and remix documents of the past with the intent of critique. These are poems that have something to say about Society with a capital S.

The term "documentary" was coined in 1926 by filmmaker John Grierson to describe the film *Moana*—not the Disney movie, but a romanticized account of life in Samoa directed by Robert J. Flaherty. By the 1930s, alongside a rise in photojournalism and documentary photography, a number of poets were writing works that would later be categorized as documentary poetry. The most well-known of these works, "The Book of the Dead," was written by Muriel Rukeyser and published in her book *U.S. 1* in 1938. In addition to being a poet, Rukeyser was a journalist and leftist activist, and in "The Book of the Dead" she turned her journalistic eye to what is still one of the largest industrial catastrophes in US history. The West Virginia Hawk's Nest Tunnel disaster involved a hydroelectric dam project of the early 1930s, in which more than seven hundred miners died after extensive exposure to silica. Union Carbide, the project's parent company, was well aware of the toxicity of the silica dust, but it required the men, who were mostly poor African Americans, to work ten-to-fifteen-hour shifts in tunnels. The tunnels were not adequately ventilated, and Union Carbide did not provide the miners with safety gear. Before I read Rukeyser's poem, I had never heard of these men or their deaths.

Rukeyser chronicles the catastrophe and its aftermath in her long poem. She incorporates testimonies from surviving families, documents from legal cases, and even information about the value of Union Carbide's stocks into the poem, which also includes more traditional forms of lyric poetry. The poem, an investigative work, sheds light on a story that the press had largely ignored; it's a form of activism against deadly labor conditions. By investigating this story through poetry rather than traditional journalism, Rukeyser was able to approach the event imaginatively and critically, to critique Union Carbide's rising stock prices by juxtaposing them with lies lyrically stated: "The dam is safe. / A scene of power. / The dam is the father of the tunnel." The dam was not safe at all, but Union Carbide did just fine on the market.

Rukeyser was not the only poet of her generation to create documentary poems. In his 1945 poem

"Middle Passage," Robert Hayden tells stories of the Atlantic slave trade, particularly the story of the slave rebellion on the *Amistad*, by incorporating legal documents into his poem. Charles Reznikoff's book *Holocaust* (1975), which was published the year before the poet's death, tells stories of the genocide of millions by lineating testimony from the Nuremberg and Eichmann trials. What makes these documentary poems—and not just poems about historical events—is that they incorporate documents themselves. They include evidence. They say: look at the historical record. Horrific events—the Atlantic slave trade, the Hawk's Nest Tunnel disaster, the Holocaust—happened. Here is our evidence.

Theodor Adorno famously wrote in "Cultural Criticism and Society" (1949) that "to write poetry after Auschwitz is barbaric." The poets I discuss in this next section—M. NourbeSe Philip, Layli Long Soldier, and J. Michael Martinez—would disagree. Through writing documentary poems that expose, engage, rewrite, and ultimately resist dominant narratives of official (which is also to say, white) documentation of history, all three poets show that engaging with world historical traumas through poetry is not barbaric, but necessary to tell stories that have not been told or, more likely, stories that have been marginalized or ignored. By engaging history aesthetically, poetry can be a means of speaking back to whitewashed histories.

* * *

Students tend to think about history as objective and art as subjective. In 2020, I taught a class that tried to follow Hong's lead in considering how and when that divide doesn't hold. My class, "Poetry as Resistance: Remixing the Archive," took up North American experimental poets of color who build their poetry around historical documents, archives, and museum holdings to resist the politics of the present moment. I had two goals for the class. First, I wanted my students to read and learn about some really excellent political poetry, much of which had been written in the past five years. Second, I wanted my students to learn how to do primary source research, to have the experience of encountering all sorts of historical documents, artifacts, and pieces of art firsthand, to get a chance to create knowledge through encounters with material culture. We were reading documentary poets who incorporated the holdings of archives and museums into their work, and by the end of the class, my students were to do the same through their own creative research projects.

I had grand visions of field trips when I began dreaming up this class, but because it was held during the COVID-19 pandemic, all of our visits to museums and archives happened virtually. We read and talked about poems, visited museums and archives from our tiny Zoom corners of the world. I signed into class twice per week from the corner of my bedroom, my small dog always visible to my students as she slept on the pillows behind my head. Despite—or maybe even because of—these very strange circumstances, it was a very good class. Sometimes you teach a particular class of students at a particular time and something special happens and you all know it. This was one of those classes.

We began the course with two essays. Cathy Park Hong's essay "Delusions of Whiteness in the Avant-Garde" helped us understand the historical exclusion of poets of color from experimental poetry movements. Then we read one of my favorite essays ever written about poetry, Audre Lorde's "Poetry Is Not a Luxury," which I quoted from in the introduction. This essay insists that, for Black women, "poetry is a vital necessity of existence"; it explains that "poetry is the way we help give name to the nameless so it can be thought." In addition to being an articulation of the self, Lorde writes that poetry can be revolutionary: "the Black Mother within each of us—the poet—whispers in our dreams: I feel, therefore I can be free. Poetry coins the language to express and charter this revolutionary demand, the implementation of that freedom." At this particular moment in time, I think that Lorde's words resonated deeply with my students. Our class held conversations about poetry's engagement with history and its political possibilities in the fourth year of the Trump presidency, in the wake of the murder of George Floyd and the nationwide protests that lasted months, while wildfires burned across California, with the COVID-19 pandemic raging. Documentary poetry in this moment felt vital.

One of the first books of poetry that we read was *Zong!* (2008), by M. NourbeSe Philip, a Canadian lawyer turned experimental poet who was born in Trinidad and Tobago. The book reckons with the 1781 massacre on the *Zong* slave ship. The ship was traveling from West Africa to the Caribbean with hundreds of enslaved people on board. The captain made serious navigational errors that slowed down the journey, and the ship was running out of food and water. The crew worried that many aboard would die of thirst and starvation on the journey and that the Gregsons (the owners of the ship) would lose money if too many more of the enslaved people died. If the enslaved people died "natural" deaths—as if there could be anything natural about enslaving and starving people—the Gregsons would not receive the insurance payout. But because the enslaved Africans were considered legal property, the Gregsons *could* make an insurance claim for lost property if the Africans drowned. And so the ship's crew decided to throw the enslaved Africans overboard. They massacred over 130 people for insurance money.

How does one tell the story of such a horrific event? What words are even appropriate to describe it? These are the animating questions of Philip's book of poetry. And Philip, at least at first, does not tell the story as I just did. When you open a copy of *Zong!* and turn to the first page of poems, you find this first half of the first poem:

Zong! #1

w w w   w   a   wa
                w   a   w a   t
er   wa   s
        our   wa
te   r gg   g   g   go
        o   oo   goo   d
            waa   wa wa
w w waa
                ter   o   oh
    on   o   ne   w one
                        w o n   d d d
        ey   d   a
    dey   a   ah   ay
            s   one   day s
                wa   wa

_____

Masuz Zuwena Ogunsheye Ziyad Ogwambi Keturah

Letters and words are strewn across the page of this and most of the poems in this book. Confronting Philip's language challenges the reader: do the usual rules of reading apply? Do we read from left to right? Top to bottom? Are we supposed to connect all of these letters and turn them into words? This is a kind of poetry that the *New England Primer* could not have prepared us to read. When I taught *Zong!* that fall, my students asked these questions and, attempting to answer them, we listened to an audio recording of Philip performing the poem. When she reads "Zong! #1" aloud, Philip enunciates each of the letters on the page slowly and carefully. She speaks from her gut and her utterances reverberate. Her performance of the poem opens up, even transforms the text for us: in Philip's voice, the "w w w" of the opening line sounds like the speech of someone parched, calling out for water. Later moments of the poem sound like someone drowning and gasping for air. After listening to Philip's performance, which takes several long minutes, we sat in silence with it for some time and then slowly made connections between the fractured words on the page and what we heard in the audio recording. We asked questions about representation and embodiment: how can a poet represent the horrific deaths of over 130 people? What words could possibly be enough? We found that in Philip's incomplete utterances and sounds that mimic the sounds of people struggling to breathe while drowning that "Zong! #1" offers one way to represent these deaths.

In the back of Philip's book, you'll find an essay called "Notanda," where Philip explains that all of the language in the poems comes from a single English legal document: the *Gregson v. Gilbert* insurance case. After the massacre upon the *Zong*, a jury found the insurers (the Gilberts) liable and ordered them to compensate the Gregsons for their property losses (the value of the enslaved people who were massacred). The insurers appealed this decision, and the legal document that Philip prints in the back of the book is the decision by three judges that the case should get a new hearing. There is no evidence that a trial ever happened. There is no evidence, either, that anyone on the crew was tried for the murders of over 130 people.

The poem takes something supposedly rational—a legal document—and fractures and fragments it; it turns the historical legal words into incoherent jumbles on the page. It obscures them by taking them out of the racist context that legally legitimated them; parts of *Zong!* later in the book are almost illegible. In her essay, Philip explains that "the disorder, logic, and irrationality of the *Zong!* poems can no more tell the story than the legal report of *Gregson v. Gilbert* masquerading as order, logic, and rationality. In their very disorder and illogic is the non-telling of the story that must be told." In her fragmented poetry and in her essay, Philip displays the insufficiency of language to convey the horror of an event like the *Zong* massacre. She resists any sort of totalizing narrative and instead exposes the limitations of poetry and language more generally. It's a poem about what poetry can't do.

I taught *Zong!* many times before the fall of 2020, but Philip's writing about the "masquerade" of rationality resonated in new ways in this class. I think many of us were trying to make sense of the not unrelated horrors of our particular moment, as the police killings of George Floyd, Breonna Taylor, Rayshard Brooks, Daniel Prude, and so many other Black Americans in 2020 filled our newsfeeds, timelines, and airwaves, and many of us filled the streets in protest. We discussed the connections between the *Zong* massacre and Derek Chauvin's murder of George Floyd, the connections between the Atlantic slave trade in which white people enslaved millions of Africans over the course of hundreds of years, and the outsized number of Black people in the United States carceral system, the largest official prison system in the world. By creating poetry out of a legal document by and about white people arguing over the question of whether or not Black people count as property, Philip exposes the violence and illogic that undergirds the entire project of chattel slavery and its aftermath, violence that was papered over with documents such as *Gregson v. Gilbert.* Just as Solmaz Sharif exposes the violence of the US military by using alphabetized words from the military dictionary in "Safe House," Philip exposes the violence of the very language of whiteness that argues about insurance technicalities and not the murder of over 130 people in *Zong!*

In this class, my students learned to question historical records of all sorts. Through poetry, we could see how official documents have a way of retroactively sanitizing an event and learned that we need to interrogate our historical documents and not take them at face value. This is exactly what Kenneth Goldsmith did *not* do in his performance in 2015. One of the things that Goldsmith failed to understand that night was that uncritically re-presenting history in a new context has a way of repeating the original trauma. Another was that his own whiteness was not a neutral subject position from which he could "objectively" relay information about Michael Brown's murder. What *Zong!* shows us is that poetry, and in particular documentary poetry, is capable of making a critique though engaging and transforming (not simply re-presenting) historical documents. Where Goldsmith reinflicts the trauma of Brown's death by repeating the historical record, Philip undermines the white version of history by reanimating the Black lives that were lost to the violence of white people. *Zong!* is a book of horror, commensurate with the actual horrors "of the story that must be told."

* * *

We read a lot of difficult texts in "Poetry as Resistance," and their difficulty was often a topic of conversation. When teaching experimental poetry, I like to start discussions of a new poem or book of poems by identifying just what makes it difficult to read or understand. It's easy to be intimidated by poems, and this exercise has a way of loosening everyone up. If we admit we don't understand something right up front, and then we identify what and how and why we don't understand it, we are well on our way to understanding. When my students and I read *Zong!*, we discussed how difficulty arises in the way Philip fragments and distorts language, how she arranges words and letters across a page, how she resists turning her poems about an event into any kind of narrative of that event. And we also discussed the way *Zong!* gives us (some) of the information we needed to interpret it in the essay that Philip included with her poems.

But we also often faced a different kind of difficulty in this class, which was our own unknowingness. "Why didn't we learn this in school?" was a constraint refrain of the class and something we talked about quite often. It's a question familiar to many of the documentary poets we were reading: why don't more of us in the United States know our histories and how we got to be where we are today? Layli Long Soldier takes up these questions directly in her book of poems *Whereas*. A citizen of the Oglala Lakota nation, Long Soldier has often been asked this question by well-meaning white people. In her book, she recounts explaining Native schools and systems of government to two white women: "They dig in they unearth the golden question My God how come we were never taught this in our schools? The concern and furrow." Throughout the book, Long Soldier shows her frustration with the lack of knowledge that most people in the US have of Native nations, people, and history. Her poetry fills in those gaps, even as doing so generates frustrations of its own.

Long Soldier's poem "38," for example, tells the story of the Dakota 38, a group of Native American men who were executed by hanging at the order of Abraham Lincoln after the Sioux Uprising. Lincoln issued this order during the same week that he signed the Emancipation Proclamation. I didn't know about the Dakota 38 before reading *Whereas*, and neither did any of my students this fall. This would come as no surprise to Long Soldier, who writes the poem in a knowing and didactic tone: "The signing of the Emancipation Proclamation was included in the film *Lincoln*; the hanging of the Dakota 38 was not. / In any case, you might be asking, 'Why were thirty-eight Dakota men hung?'" Throughout the book, Long Soldier positions herself as an educator of Americans who should know better but don't. She feels deeply ambivalent about this role but takes it on anyway.

I was teaching Long Soldier's poems at a large public university in California in a class that was diverse by every metric that one might use to measure diversity other than age. The majority of my students were people of color, and I wondered what their experiences were with learning the histories of Indigenous peoples of North America. I knew what my K–12 education had been like in a very white town on the East Coast in the 1980s and 1990s: deeply flawed and often inaccurate. My students were fifteen to twenty years younger than I was, and I was curious if they had been educated about Native histories differently. It turns out, they had not, and they had quite a bit to say on the topic, particularly about their "mission projects." Until 2017—when activists finally succeeded in getting the state curriculum changed—fourth-grade students across California undertook "mission projects" in which they learned about the late eighteenth-century missions set up by Spanish priests to "civilize" and convert the Native peoples to Catholicism. They built arts-and-crafts models of the missions, they took field trips to them, and everyone involved made the mission period sound like a grand old time in which white settlers taught important lessons to Indigenous peoples and everyone got along swimmingly. Most of my students knew, by the time they reached college, that what they had learned in their mission projects were downright lies, that the missions were violent and oppressive institutions in which priests rounded up Native peoples, stripped them of their customs and ways of life, forced them into Christianity, and required them to labor. The Spanish killed tens of thousands of the people of the West Coast through the missions and the epidemics that they brought with them.

Long Soldier is a citizen of the Oglala Lakota Nation, located in South Dakota, which is definitely not California, and I don't want to conflate all Native peoples and histories together. The missions of California are not part of Long Soldier's personal history. But the "mission projects" were my (mostly) Californian students' entry point into histories of Indigenous people in the US. It felt important to me, in this classroom setting in which we read so many poems by poets interested in correcting historical records, to articulate what we have learned and from where we have learned it, to acknowledge our own ignorance so that we could work to overcome it. Documentary poems created a space for these conversations, and for our learning.

One of the many things that my students learned from Long Soldier is that the US government made an official apology to Native Americans. The second part of the book *Whereas*—also titled "Whereas"— comprises a long documentary poem about this apology. In her introduction, Long Soldier explains that Barack Obama signed the Congressional Resolution of Apology to Native Americans in 2009. It was an official moment of recognition of what white people have done to Indigenous peoples, but the Apology is totally, woefully, insufficient, full of euphemisms and obfuscations. No tribal representatives were invited to acknowledge the Apology in any way, and Obama never read the resolution aloud publicly. It is unclear what it was trying to accomplish, other than making non-Indigenous Americans feel better about themselves. In her book, Long Soldier explains that the poem "Whereas" responds directly to "the Apology's delivery, as well as the language, crafting, and arrangement of the written document." In the sections that follow, Long Soldier examines this document closely; she incorporates quotes from it into some sections, addresses it indirectly in others, and, taking a page from *Zong!*, fractures, fragments, and reconstitutes it otherwise in others. "Whereas" is an exquisite undermining of the Apology at every turn.

One of the sections of the long poem addresses the Apology head-on. Long Soldier intertwines a scene of her reading of the statement with a story of her daughter suffering from a minor injury. Long Soldier doesn't reprint the full text of the Apology in her book, but she frequently incorporates phrases from it. The poem begins with the speaker reading the Apology: "WHEREAS my eyes land on the shoreline of 'the arrival of Europeans in North America opened a new chapter in the history of Native Peoples.' Because in others, I hate the act / of laughing when hurt injured or in cases of danger. That bitter hiding." Long Soldier's speaker—a figure of the poet—dramatizes her reading of the statement, telling us that her eyes "land on the shoreline" of its fifth "whereas" statement. The actual 2009 statement reads: "the arrival of Europeans in North America opened a new chapter in the history of Native Peoples." The statement provokes a strong reaction in the speaker, and I will say what Long Solider doesn't: that this "new chapter in the history of Native Peoples" might more accurately be described as *genocide*. In these opening lines, then, Long Soldier acknowledges the Apology's euphemisms and subverts a particular fantasy of settler colonialism: the peaceful arrival of Europeans on the shores of North America. Her documentary poem speaks back to the original, misleading document. The poet creates a space for herself within the Apology. She arrives on *its* shoreline and colonizes it.

But instead of correcting the Apology's many inaccuracies directly, Long Soldier makes a more subtle critique by intertwining her scene of reading with the story of an injury that her daughter suffers. The poem continues:

> . . . My daughter picks up
> new habits from friends. She'd been running,
>   tripped, slid on knees and palms onto asphalt.
>
> They carried her into the kitchen, *she just fell,*
>   *she's bleeding*! Deep red streams
> down her arms and legs, trails on white tile. I
>   looked at her face. A smile

quivered her. A laugh, a nervous. Doing as her
    friends do, she braved new behavior, feigned
a grin—I couldn't name it but I could spot it.
    Stop, my girl. If you're hurting, cry.

Like that. She let it out, a flood from living room
    to bathroom. Then a soft water pour
I washed carefully light touch clean cotton to
    bandage. I faced her I reminded,

In our home in our family we are ourselves, real
    feelings. Be true. Yet I'm serious
when I say I laugh reading the phrase, "opened a
    new chapter." I can't help my body.

I shake. The realization that it took this phrase to
    show. My daughter's quiver isn't new—
but a deep practice very old she's watching me;

The speaker's daughter has shown up at home with
skinned knees and palms; she tries to swallow her
pain with laughter, presumably to impress her friends.
The speaker of the poem tells us that she "hate[s]
the act of laughing when hurt injured or in cases of
danger. That bitter hiding," and she encourages her
daughter to let herself cry. Her daughter does.

But the speaker doesn't take her own advice. When
she reads the line from the Apology about "a new
chapter" for Native peoples, she writes, "Yet I'm seri-

ous / when I say I laugh," and that she "can't help [her] body." The Apology's absurdity makes the speaker laugh and shake, and her daughter's small bloody body is a stark reminder of what happened in this "new chapter" of settler colonialism. The "deep red streams / down her arms and legs" in the poem stand in for the deaths of millions of Native people at the hands of white settlers. This blood and the "flood" of her daughter's tears stand in for hundreds of years of death and suffering. The speaker may laugh instead of cry, but her daughter's "real feelings" let us know just what Long Soldier thinks of Obama's Apology and its painful mischaracterization of genocide. Her daughter's tears are a substitute for her own.

In a later section of "Whereas," Long Soldier, borrowing a page from Philip, turns one of the Apology's statements into a fractured, disjointed poem. The Apology reads, "The United States, acting through Congress . . . recognizes that there have been years of official depredations, ill-conceived policies, and the breaking of covenants by the Federal Government regarding Indian tribes." Long Soldier turns that statement into an eight-line poem centered on the page with footnotes below. The poem reads, "I / recognize / that[1] / official[2] / ill-[3] / breaking of[4] / the[5] / Indian[6]." The words that have been deleted from the original Apology appear in footnotes on the bottom of the page.

The only word that Long Soldier adds to the Apology is an "I." But this change is important; in doing

(3)

I

recognize

that [1]

official [2]

ill- [3]

breaking of [4]

the [5]

Indian [6]

---

1. *there have been years of* 2. *depradations,* 3. *conceived policies, and the* 4. *covenants by*
5. *Federal Government regarding* 6. *tribes*

so, she imagines a person behind the impersonal legal language of the Apology. And this "I" makes a more meaningful apology than the US government does. The I "recognizes" what the US government cannot: "that / official / ill- / breaking of / the / Indian." Long Soldier insists on the humanity of "the / Indian," of the individual. She asks us to see that white people have broken more than a set of treaties—they have broken, or tried to break, human beings. But the words from the original statement haunt Long Soldier's poem; she prints them below the body text in footnotes. She subsumes them, but she can't escape the euphemistic and harmful language of white people no matter how much she rearranges it. And whether it comes out as a shaking laugh or a cry, the pain of her history and the politics of her present moment are real. Poetry is a form of resistance, but that doesn't mean it doesn't hurt.

* * *

Some books of documentary poems, such as *Zong!* and *Whereas*, obsess over single documents. Others, like J. Michael Martinez's *Museum of the Americas*, are more capacious. Martinez's book is aptly named; opening its pages is not unlike visiting a museum. In addition to poems, the book includes photographs, picture postcards, legal documents, treaties, and snippets of academic scholarship. By weaving together these historical items and objects along with family photographs and personal narratives, Martinez creates a book of poems probing the historical relationships of the US and Mexico and the experiences of the millions of people caught somewhere between the two nations. He understands his own body as the result of hundreds of years of imperial history, and he brings together all kinds of evidence in his book as if to say: look what I am made of. And look what I can do with it.

Museum of the Americas was one of the last books I assigned in my class, and at this point in the academic quarter, I knew what my students were capable of. Instead of telling them everything I wanted them to know in order to understand and interpret Martinez's poems, I split the class into groups, assigned each group a few poems, and then sent them all to Zoom breakout rooms to research the many documents and artifacts incorporated into their section of the book. When they came back, their task was to tell their classmates everything they needed to "get" their poem. And they returned with a rich mass of materials: images of eighteenth-century *casta* paintings, postcard photographs from the Mexican Revolution that had been widely distributed in the US, the story of the head of Joaquin Murrieta, several articles from the Treaty of Guadalupe Hidalgo, the story of the prosthetic leg of General Santa Anna, US naturalization forms, and more.

My students brought it. They came back from their breakout rooms energized and with pages of information to share. They had created their own museum of the Americas that we could use to understand Martinez's *Museum of the Americas*, and we talked through maps of the US at various points in the eighteenth and nineteenth centuries. We read sections of treaties, looked at postcards and paintings that Martinez had referenced in his book but not included in it. In doing this research activity, my students actively created knowledge for themselves. And, using the knowledge they had gained from the poets they had read, they looked at the documents that they had assembled critically, thinking both about their context and the positionality of their authors.

One of Martinez's unnamed poems is about the Treaty of Guadalupe Hidalgo, the treaty between the US and Mexico that ended the Mexican-American War in 1848. (It is worth mentioning that the war is known in Mexico as "la Guerra de Estados Unidos a México," or sometimes "Intervención estadounidense en México"—the "US Intervention in Mexico.") In the treaty, the US annexed 525,000 square miles (present-day California, Nevada, Utah, and parts of Wyoming, Arizona, New Mexico, and Colorado) from Mexico. In the poem, Martinez explains that the Mexicans living in the annexed land could choose to move to Mexico; those who didn't leave were left in an ambiguous state. The treaty says that these Mexicans "shall be considered to have elected to become citizens of the United States" and that they "shall be incorporated into the Union of the United States & be admitted, at the proper time (to be judged of by the Congress of the United States)." When presenting their research, my students explained that only a few thousand people elected to move to Mexico, and most stayed put in their homeland that was now not quite theirs. Martinez is attuned to the way that the treaty left most of the Mexicans in these thousands of square miles in a liminal space, with the US government left to determine citizenship "at the right time." Later, Martinez writes:

> The Treaty of Guadalupe may be seen as not only a political treaty between countries, but as a kind of fashioned poetic of ever emergent subjectivities. Legislated without boundary, these peoples became foreign unto themselves, poltergeists of a former flesh. Neither this nor that but as visions of corporeality, in time, each traverses historical vanishing, an archive of colored flesh, naked of nation.

When my students did their research on the treaty, they shared various historical maps of the US, Mexico, and the land that the US had taken from Mexico. They shared statistics: how many people left, how many people stayed. We talked about the metaphorical connections between the Mexicans who lived on these lands and the broken body parts and prosthetics that haunt Martinez's poems. We talked about the ways that the US made whole people partial, ghostly— "poltergeists of a former flesh"— and how the aftereffects of the treaty resonate today on the US-Mexico border.

As a class, we decided that in *Museum of the Americas* Martinez creates a counter-archive to official histories and grand narratives of war and conquest that is both personal and political. He creates a place for himself, his family, his ancestors, and the millions of others who also experience *nepantla*, a term that scholars, artists, and activists use to discuss the particular form of Chicanx liminality that Martinez chronicles throughout his book. When reading Martinez and researching his poems, my students contributed to and grew this counter-archive. They helped to stay the "historical vanishing" that Martinez writes about in his poems by making meaning alongside and with them.

In other words, the difficulty of documentary poems and the demands they make on readers are part of their powerful political resistance. They demand that we understand the historical contexts of their making, that we examine the evidence that they present, and that, having seen their evidence, we work alongside them in the pursuit of justice. The difficulty in reading and grasping, I think, is the point: they demand our participation in making meaning. They ask us to do our reading actively.

* * *

On the last day of class, one of my students said, "I think we should always learn history through poetry," and it was one of those moments that I wish could replay every time someone says something disparaging about poetry, or any art form really, and its ability to do anything useful in the world. Poetry, in this class, became a means for us to think about the politics of the past and present as deeply intertwined. This question of whether or not poetry is capable of doing anything in the world has been a favorite topic of poets as long as there have been poets. The British poet W. H. Auden famously wrote that "poetry makes nothing happen" in his elegy for the Irish poet W. B. Yeats. People love to cite this quote as proof that even poets think poetry is useless for political action. But just a few lines down, he writes that "it survives, / A way of happening, a mouth." Auden, I think, would agree with Lorde: poetry is not just something one reads. It is a way of being in the world, a way of happening, an articulation of what was and what might be if we dare to speak it. It can be a revolutionary mouth for people who have historically been silenced. But, as we have also seen, for poets like Collins and Goldsmith, poetry is not always politically radical. Like all art, it is often a means of affirming the status quo. And this poetry is poetry too, even if it is not the kind of poetry that I really want to spend my time with anymore.

The final project of the class was for my students to make a creative research project of their own. I wanted them to take inspiration from the poets we read by engaging archival material that was significant to them personally and to use it to make some kind of critique. The parameters were broad, but the critique part was key; I asked my students to bring some kind of knowledge that they had from their lived experiences to bear on historical materials. And their projects were fantastic. Students made sequences of erasure poems, short documentaries, collages, zines, concrete poems, and sculptures. One student, a campus activist, turned archives of official statements made by the university about racism on campus into a series of subversive erasure poems exposing the hypocrisy of the administration. Another student dug into queer zine archives from the 1970s, and, seeing a lack of representation of bisexual people, made their own zine out of the materials from the original zines that addressed both this lack and the binaries present in queer thinking of the time. Another student created a series of poems that juxtaposed the text of the Chinese Exclusion Act of 1882 with language from newspaper headlines about COVID-19 or, as Trump is fond of calling it, the "China Flu." In creating these projects, my students were able to learn experientially, to create their own documentary forms of witnessing and critique, to merge the personal with the political, to survive, to be a mouth.

In 2020, when many of us were trying, quite literally, just to survive, documentary poems gave my students and me a way of understanding and talking about our present moment. And we used these tools to talk about not just the world outside, but ourselves. Throughout the class, I was keenly aware of my positionality—as a white woman teaching the works of poets of color to a majority non-white class, as a literary scholar, not a historian, teaching so much about history—and this was something we discussed in the virtual classroom too. Why not? The poems gave us a chance to think about the politics of all kinds of institutions, and we talked about graduate school and how one gets to be the person in front of the classroom, about who teaches college and under what conditions they get to be there.

But mostly we discussed the poems. And what I liked to remind my students is that documentary poetry asks us to look forward as well as back. As Lorde tells us, poetry helps us articulate our innermost selves: "I feel, therefore I can be free. Poetry coins the language to express and charter this revolutionary demand, the implementation of that freedom."

Documentary poetry doesn't just help us understand the past, it helps us create the futures that we want. In asking my students to make their own creative works, I hoped they could get a taste of what it feels like to make a critique, but more importantly, a demand. And while I don't imagine that my students and I dismantled white supremacy in ten weeks in the fall of 2020, I do think we learned some of the tools of subversion and resistance. This is what documentary poetry can do. It can give the historically silenced a mouth, so that they can demand more.

4

THE INTERNET POEM

To Soothe

In August 2019, a woman named Agnes walked into a public restroom in England and heard the sound of another woman crying behind a stall door. Agnes asked the woman if she was okay, if she needed anything. The woman was crying, she said, because she missed her mother, who had died. And then, while the woman peed, Agnes read her a poem—"To the Woman Crying Uncontrollably in the Next Stall," by Kim Addonizio. When Agnes finished reading, the woman asked Agnes for her number. Later that night she texted her: "I will never ever forget your voice through the closed door. Thank you Agnes xxx."

"To the Woman Crying Uncontrollably in the Next Stall" is just so apt for this bathroom moment between the two women. It begins with a direct address to a "you," a "you" who is very much the type of person who might find herself crying uncontrollably in public, a you who is perhaps a bit messy, and whose messiness the poem will detail: it begins "If you ever woke in your dress at 4am ever / closed your legs to someone you loved opened / them for someone you didn't moved against / a pillow in the dark stood miserably on a beach / seaweed clinging to your ankles." As Addonizio continues, the messiness accrues:

> . . . paid
> good money for a bad haircut backed away
> from a mirror that wanted to kill you bled
> into the back seat for lack of a tampon
> if you swam across a river under rain sang
> using a dildo for a microphone stayed up
> to watch the moon eat the sun entire
> ripped out the stitches in your heart
> because why not if you think nothing &
> no one can / listen I love you joy is coming

I read this poem and can so clearly picture Agnes reading it to the crying woman, the woman's tears only increasing at the final line.

The reason why I know this story, which may or may not be true, is not that I'm friends with Agnes, but that Agnes told the story on Twitter, where it went viral and was written up in several British publications. As you may have already surmised from reading this book, I spend a lot of time on the internet, and way too much time on Twitter. It is what it is. And when a Twitter friend first shared the Agnes story with me, I was surprised that I missed the original viral tweet thread; if something poetry related goes viral at this magnitude on Twitter, I usually manage to see it. I later went back and checked the date of the thread; the story went viral just as I arrived back in Los Angeles after three years in Maine. It was a difficult time for me, and I was trying to stay off of Twitter, which has a way of amplifying my ugliest feelings. So I will forgive myself for missing this story during this moment of personal upheaval.

In the 1990s, poems existed for me in books and in my brain and then maybe you could read them aloud to make someone fall in love with you, but that was it. Teen me could not fathom today, in which people tweet poems, share poems on Facebook, post them on Instagram and Pinterest and Tumblr, create them on TikTok. These days, poetry happens on the internet, and on social media particularly. A few Instapoets are followed by millions; many others have smaller but still huge followings (in the tens of thousands). They post poems to Instagram on a daily or weekly basis. And the internet is not just where already published poems, such as "To the Woman Crying Uncontrollably in the Next Stall" have second lives; many poems these days are created specifically for social media. Sometimes, later, they are turned into books.

I want to talk about both kinds: poems that circulate widely on social media as well as those created specifically to appear there. Earlier this year I tweeted out a question several times—what are some poems that have had interesting lives on the internet—and the poems I will be discussing here are ones many people recommended to me. Twitter is a very different institution than higher education, but it too has its poetry canons, and "To the Woman Crying Uncontrollably in the Next Stall" is very much in the Twitter poetry canon. The poem was not originally created for the internet, but it has been given a second, larger life there. It first appeared in the chapbook *The Night Could Go in Either Direction*, a collaboration between Addonizio and Brittany Perham published in 2016, the year I moved from Los Angeles to Maine. The poem's publication and its viral moment three years later bookended that period in my life. Agnes didn't explain how she came to know the poem in her viral tweets, but I'd bet a lot of money that she had seen the poem floating on the internet somewhere previously and saved the poem to her phone, or found it quickly by googling the title in the moment. I doubt that she happened to have a copy of the chapbook with her in the bathroom that day, although maybe she did, as one does when one reads poetry.

Because I will be talking about a lot of popular poems that many poetry professionals (myself included) might snub their noses at, I will just say upfront that I think "To the Woman Crying Uncontrollably in the Next Stall" is a good poem. What makes it good? It's a sonnet that knows the rules and history of the form and how to play with them. It has a distinct voice. Addonizio almost completely omits punctuation and conjunctions in the poem, so when you read it aloud the lines come out of your mouth like a rush of air. The phrases spill from one line to another and create interesting enjambments that often leave verbs hanging on the ends of lines. The poem's repetitions are pleasing, structured, so that, like many of the sonnets I discussed, it takes the form of a litany. The poem also has a perfect, very late— in-the-middle-of-line-14 late—volta, which I will say more about in just a bit. For now, let's just say that Addonizio knows her way around the sonnet form. She knows what the traditions of the form are, what other poets have done with it, and she makes it her own. These are things that I, as someone trained in poetry, admire. I could teach this poem.

The poem is a litany of many things that many women have done: cried, bled, fucked the wrong people, paid good money for a bad haircut. These common experiences aren't particularly bound by things like race or class or age, though of course how the speaker feels about having done these things surely is. As for me, I have done most of the things that Addonizio lists in her poem. When Addonizio writes "you," I feel addressed by it, and not just because the speaker addresses the poem to a "you" who is both the woman crying uncontrollably in the next stall and a more general "you" who is the reader of the poem. (This is how second person addresses often work in poems; they are addressed both to a singular person within the space of the poem and to a more generalized audience.) When I read the poem, I feel more like that singular person rather than that general audience, because I am someone who has cried uncontrollably in public: in bathrooms, yes, but also on park benches and on the subway, in classrooms and once at Ralph's when Adele's "Someone Like You" came on the loudspeaker while I was in the middle of a breakup. It's what yearners do. The poem speaks to me. And as it moves through its fourteen lines, it becomes less of a list of things that women have done or experienced and it becomes increasingly metaphorical; instead of bleeding in the backseat of a car or using a dildo as a microphone, Addonizio speaks to you who have "stayed up / to watch the moon eat the sun" and "ripped out the stitches in your heart." The poem becomes more, well, poetic (hello, moon—did you come from my first college sonnet?), and then moves into abstraction: "why not if you think nothing & / no one can." And then the poem turns at that perfect, mid-line volta that addresses you directly: "listen I love you joy is coming."

I cried when I read this poem in the context of Agnes's viral Twitter thread. I had read it previously and not cried, but when it was embedded in the story it was too much, and, sitting on the couch in my pajamas on a Sunday afternoon with no one to see me but my dog, I burst into tears at my laptop. The way the poem stages that moment of acknowledgment, of being seen and understood and affirmed? And then the way it actually happened between two strangers, one caring for the other in real life? Just like in the poem?

I think about the difference between this viral moment and the viral moment of Idusuyi reading *Citizen* at the Trump rally in 2015. In both moments, poetry turned out to be instrumental. Idusuyi's reading electrified a collective mass audience; it gave us something to pay attention to, to delight in, to support, to distract us from the bloviating racist on stage. It was, in a way, a form of care: of Idusuyi taking care of herself in a terrible situation, which translated to a more collective form of care of a wider American audience. Agnes's bathroom moment was a form of care too, on a smaller, more tender scale. It soothed an individual and then it soothed me. Sometimes you (I) just need to hear "joy is coming" and sometimes when someone tells you (me) that it is in fact coming, you (I) cry, because after spending more than a year alone in a small apartment trying not to die of a deadly pandemic, it seems like it might be possible for the first time in a long time.

After this experience, and knowing that I was going to write about "To the Woman Crying Uncontrollably in the Next Stall," I shared the poem with friends who are poetry readers and friends who are not at all poetry readers and asked them what they thought about it. Some found the poem trite. More than one suggested that it sounds like it was written by a teenage girl. Others said it was clearly written *for* teenage girls, probably straight white teenage girls, and thus it was not for them. (I do not disagree.) Others found it just fine but not particularly moving. Two friends, friends who know their way around a poem, felt as strongly as I did, and especially about the volta, about that "listen" that speaks to "you" directly, maybe even just a tiny bit harshly, which may be exactly what you need sometimes. Both of these friends, who are also friends with each other, had seen the poem before. One had shared it with the other ages ago. Both are writers, young, and messy. I know at least one of them has cried in public plenty, because we have talked about it. We are like each other in a lot of ways, except I am not exactly young anymore. But I think we are of a kind, and I think "To the Woman Crying Uncontrollably in the Next Stall" is a poem for the young and messy, or for those who have been young and messy, for those of us who are, perhaps, still messy in particular kinds of teenage ways.

"To the Woman Crying Uncontrollably in the Next Stall" offers a balm, and that's what it shares with other poems that live on the internet, the ones I'll talk about here. They are poems for you to read to yourself—alone at your device reaching toward the social of the internet—when you are sad or angry at the world or frustrated or lonely. They will try to see you and soothe you and they will not be ironic about it. I talked to a lot of people (many of whom are not regular poetry readers) to get their input on these poems. When you get a PhD in literature as I did, when you focus on modernism, you don't read a lot of poems that try to make you feel good. This is especially true when you spend your undergraduate and graduate careers writing seminar papers on T. S. Eliot's *The Waste Land*, which I am pretty sure is supposed to make you feel terrible. I have spent a lot of my life reading poems about how terrible life is, and generally these are the poems I find meaningful and intellectually and politically valuable. Poems that occlude the terribleness of everything often feel disingenuous to me. And Billy Collins's comforting of Dick Cheney makes me want to barf.

I do have poets I read when I am looking to feel nourished in some way—Frank O'Hara, Anne Carson—but I don't think their poems care about my needs at all. Their poems may make me feel better, or make me laugh, or make me feel like I am among my likeminded poetry weirdos, but they are not written with the express purpose of soothing me. The internet poems I'm interested in here are. They are instrumental. They do not pretend that the world is not terrible, but they do want you to find a calm place in it from which to thrive. For this reason, among others, many poets, critics, and scholars find these internet poems banal and trite. My instinct is to also find them banal and trite, but I am trying to put these judgments aside, to see these poems for what they are: not experimental works that push the boundaries of language and sense and politics (my preference) but poems to read at the end of a long day when you might want to be seen or comforted or validated, because the rest of the terrible world isn't doing that for you. I was trained in graduate school to see poems as the expression of anything but care. What if I tried to read them otherwise?

Aesthetic judgment feels more complicated for me now. I used to say things like "this is a good poem" and "this is a bad poem" all of the time to classrooms full of people who wrote down what I said and maybe went on to adopt my judgments as their own. I'm trying to do that less now, trying to see in poems what other people see. And no matter how I choose to read and interpret them, internet poems are worth reading and thinking about for their popularity alone. When Khloé Kardashian posts a poem by Instapoet r.m. drake to her 189 million followers, it is getting a lot more attention than any poem by my beloved modernist poet Mina Loy probably ever has or will. Poetry, for most people, is something between a Hallmark card from the 1980s and a "LIVE LAUGH LOVE" sign. We—and this is a big we here, as it includes Khloé Kardashian and Rupi Kaur's 4.4 million Instagram followers—turn to internet poems in times of need: after a death, after a breakup, during a war, throughout a pandemic. Internet poems are the voice of Agnes reading to us from the next stall over in the public bathroom, telling us what we need to hear when we need it. They tell us "listen

I love you joy is coming" when we think we might never feel love or joy again.

* * *

Unlike sonnets, alphabet poems (well, abecedarians), and documentary poems, there is no definition for internet poems in the *Princeton Encyclopedia of Poetry and Poetics*, the place that you might go for that sort of thing. Instead, I use the term "internet poem" to refer to poems of all sorts that have circulated widely on the internet. They may be created especially for a social media outlet (like the poems of Rupi Kaur and Instagram), or they may be poems first published in print journals, magazines, chapbooks, or books (like "To the Woman Crying Uncontrollably in the Next Stall") that have had second or third lives on Instagram or Pinterest, in email inboxes or on Twitter. It is a term that has to do with circulation, not with form. And while not all internet poems try to make us feel better about ourselves or our worlds, a large number of them do, especially those that are created specifically for social media. These are the internet poems that interest me.

The one formal feature that many internet poems share is that they are almost always short. Internet poems are rarely more than twenty lines, because it is hard to fit an image on an Instagram grid that is more than twenty lines. Also, people have short attention spans. This is also why people like sonnets.

The shorter a poem is, the better, as far as popularity goes. In addition to being short, internet poems are accessible. They don't demand with their form or content. You may need a guide, or some context, or at least a lot of time to read an experimental book of poetry such as Philip's *Zong!*; this is not the case with internet poems. They use accessible language. You can scroll through them and digest them quickly. They often create intimacy through an address to a "you." They intend to catch you right away. There are many reasons not to like internet poems, but it's not because of your lack of comprehension, which is often a reason that people don't like (or are afraid to like, or don't want to put in the effort to like) poems more generally. Unlike the documentary poems I discussed earlier, internet poems are easy to read, and they go easy on you.

When I asked Twitter about poems that have had interesting lives on the internet, Maggie Smith's "Good Bones," Ross Gay's "A Small Needful Fact," and Mary Oliver's "Wild Geese" were the poems that came up again and again. The first two of these poems were written in the mid-2010s, while Oliver's poem was written in the 1980s. Each of these poems tries to soothe a different hurt, a hurt that is personal or political or both. "Good Bones" was written by poet Maggie Smith (not to be confused with Dame Maggie Smith) and first published in the online *Waxwing* literary journal in 2016, a few days after the mass shooting at the Pulse nightclub in Orlando. The poem quickly began to circulate across social media in posts and tweets related to the massacre, and it continues to circulate widely every time something horrific happens in the United States, which is frequently. I first saw it on social media in the wake of Trump's election, when it was all over Twitter and Instagram. The poem begins:

> Life is short, though I keep this from my
>   children.
> Life is short, and I've shortened mine
> in a thousand delicious, ill-advised ways,
> a thousand deliciously ill-advised ways
> I'll keep from my children. The world is at least
> fifty percent terrible, and that's a conservative
> estimate, though I keep this from my children.

This poem, like a good therapist, acknowledges your feelings about the world being terrible. It does not try to convince you that you are not feeling what you're feeling, and it appreciates the difficulties of parenting within a terrible world. Life is terrible but also it is short, and you may have even contributed to its shortness through your "delicious, ill-advised ways." (Your ways are so delicious, and so ill-advised, we must hear about them twice.)

As the poem continues, it leans into all of the ways the world is terrible. It does not hold back:

For every bird there is a stone thrown at a bird.
For every loved child, a child broken, bagged,
sunk in a lake. Life is short and the world
is at least half terrible, and for every kind
stranger, there is one who would break you,
though I keep this from my children. I am trying
to sell them the world. Any decent realtor,
walking you through a real shithole, chirps on
about good bones: This place could be beautiful,
right? You could make this place beautiful.

As we can see, in the final few lines, the poem shifts. Yes, the world is terrible, but the speaker tells us that she is trying to "sell" her children the world. And she imagines a realtor trying to sell "a real shithole" of a house, while saying that the home has "good bones": "This place could be beautiful, / right? You could make this place beautiful."

As I have discovered in writing about "Good Bones," this poem has its proponents and its detractors. Here I will confess: I am one of its detractors. It irks me. I do not like the ending, the idea that the world has "good bones," and that, like a shithole of a house, it can be spiffed up with a new en suite bathroom or a large marble kitchen island because its problems are cosmetic. It is my instinct to read this poem judgmentally, eye-rollingly. I should also say now, and I think this is important: I am not a parent. And neither were the students in my "Poetry as Resistance" course with whom I shared the poem. None of them had seen the poem before, which suggests to me that though it may circulate widely on my elder millennial internet, it has not done the same on the younger millennial/Gen Z–cusp internet. My students did not like the poem. One student said they thought that this is a poem for old people who rely on younger generations to fix their mistakes. Another said that this country does not have good bones, that it has shit for bones, and if the world is so shitty why wait for your children to fix it while you are having fun in your "ill-advised ways"? They said it was a selfish poem. I laughed. I will add to these Gen Z critiques the critique of an elder millennial: the realtor metaphor may not speak to as many people as Maggie Smith would like to think. And neither does the idea of keeping your children from understanding the terrors of the world. This seems like a particular fantasy reserved for white people who, for example, may not have to warn their children about interacting with the police from a young age just to keep them alive.

But I have also talked to parents about this poem, parents who feel the poem speaks to them. One Gen X parent countered my snarky reading of the poem by telling me that she doesn't believe that the poem believes in the real estate agent's promise about good bones at all, that this is not a hopeful poem, but a poem about despair. That this is a poem that acknowledges the incalculable damage that humans have done to the world, that the realtor's chirping about "good bones" rings hollow, that it is a terrible feeling to try to sell your children the world, knowing how we have trashed it, and knowing that their lives will probably not be as good as their parents'. Parents are not calmed by this poem with bland hopes for a white subway tile backsplash that will revive the shithole world, but seen and affirmed by the way the poem freely admits how terrible it all is. What I learned from all of these conversations about "Good Bones" is something that I didn't think too much about at first when it comes to internet poems but now seems glaringly obvious when it comes to internet poems (or indeed any poems at all): whether or not you are soothed by a poem has everything to do with who you are and whether or not the poem was written with (someone like) you in mind.

I don't remember when I first read Ross Gay's poem "A Small Needful Fact," but I do remember my reaction to seeing it on a friend's Instagram account during the summer of 2020 in the midst of the Black Lives Matter protests, which was: wow. That "wow" was not about the poem itself; it was about the fact that that particular friend was sharing a poem at all. "A Small Needful Fact" was clearly speaking to a wide range of people. The poem was first published in 2015 on *Split This Rock*, a website for socially engaged poets and their work. It is an elegy for Eric Garner, who was killed in the summer of 2014 by police officer Daniel Pantaleo after Pantaleo put Garner in a chokehold while arresting him. Garner repeatedly said "I can't breathe" as he was dying. The statement became one of the rallying cries of the Black Lives Matter movement.

"A Small Needful Fact" circulates on social media time and time again when a police officer kills a Black person in the United States. It was all over my social media during the worldwide protests after Derek Chauvin's killing of George Floyd in 2020. Though the poem is specifically about Garner, it has come to stand in for many of the other Black victims of police violence in the years since it was first published. "A Small Needful Fact" is both the title and the first line of the poem. It is followed by the statement of that fact: "Is that Eric Garner worked / for some time for the Parks and Rec. / Horticultural Department." This is a simple declarative statement. But the poem then takes a more imaginative turn with a set of conditional statements:

> . . . . which means,
> perhaps, that with his very large hands,
> perhaps, in all likelihood,
> he put gently into the earth
> some plants which, most likely,
> some of them, in all likelihood,
> continue to grow, continue
> to do what such plants do, like house
> and feed small and necessary creatures,
> like being pleasant to touch and smell,
> like converting sunlight
> into food, like making it easier
> for us to breathe.

Gay's poem imagines that "perhaps" Garner planted some plants in this job that "in all likelihood / continue to grow" and that these plants are still living their plant-y lives and emitting oxygen through photosynthesis even today. Garner may not be with us, but his (imagined and probable) plants remain and make it "easier / for us to breathe."

To feel the full effect of the poem, we must know that Garner's final words were "I can't breathe." It's a lower hurdle for understanding than, say, knowing the details of the *Gregson v. Gilbert* case in Philips's *Zong!*, as Garner's words have been plastered across protest signs and on social media for years. The poem's power lies in the irony that Garner's breath was stolen from him, but that in Gay's imaginings, Garner's labor provides oxygen for those who outlive him. The poem is an elegy that laments the dead— Garner's large hands, his gentleness and careful work—but also imports a larger significance to his life. His breath was stolen, but he makes it "easier / for us to breathe." That is a big "us" there. And while I do not want to suggest that "A Small Needful Fact" is a joyful poem, I do think that, like other internet poems, and unlike many other poems about the police killings of Black people in the United States, there is something hopeful about it. Garner is still with us, through his plants, but also, if we are going to read more expansively, through another form of his legacy: the Black Lives Matter movement, through all of us who hold "I can't breathe" signs and say his name at protests.

"A Small Needful Fact" is an affirming poem about Garner's life, not his death, and I think it can circulate so widely because it eschews politics of any kind while centering the person who was killed. It doesn't consider the how and why of Garner's death, nor the by whom. When asked about the poem, Gay said, "What that poem, I think, is trying to do is to say, there's this beautiful life, which is both the sorrow and the thing that needs to be loved." This is a poem that insists on care, legacy, and regeneration. These are powerful messages for a community trying to sustain itself in the face of state-sanctioned violence. The generosity of its final "us," though, allows those who don't face that violence also to stand in its shelter, which is why it can be so widely loved, and why, sometimes, I think white readers sharing this poem are accepting a soothing they have not earned.

Unlike "Good Bones" and "A Small Needful Fact," Mary Oliver's poem "Wild Geese," which was first published in her 1986 book *Dream Work*, does not seem to circulate on social media with a particular political catalyst. The poem is about the inner self, which I guess is always relevant. Oliver died in 2019 and had a long career of writing bestselling poetry books. She won both the National Book Award and the Pulitzer Prize for her writing, but she has never been of much interest to poetry scholars. Once, I saw a modern poetry professor, someone senior and important in the field, hold up one of Oliver's poems as an example of a bad poem during a talk. I can't say I didn't laugh as I watched the professor tear the poem apart and make fun of its line breaks. (This is what counts as a good time in academia.) I have never been a fan of Oliver's, but I have long suspected that this was for personal as well as professional reasons. I will explain.

While doing some research on Oliver, I found that there were many references to her books in academic articles, but not from the field of literature. She is frequently quoted in articles on cognitive behavioral therapy, on mindfulness, in workbooks on trauma. Her poems have been instrumentalized by the field of psychology. This tracks with where I see them on the internet: on self-helpy, health and wellness-y, inspirational white lady corners of social media. I have it on good authority that yoga teachers often read her poems aloud in class. When Oliver died in 2019, Gwyneth Paltrow posted "Wild Geese" on her Instagram grid. The poem begins:

> You do not have to be good.
> You do not have to walk on your knees
> for a hundred miles through the desert,
>   repenting.
> You only have to let the soft animal of your body
>   love what it loves.
> Tell me about despair, yours, and I will tell you
>   mine.

From the very beginning, the poem addresses "you" and tells you to go easier on yourself. You do not have to be perfect. You do not even have to be good. You do not have to punish yourself. We are all in pain and we can talk about it. And while we are talking about it, the world keeps moving and doing its thing:

> Meanwhile the world goes on.
> Meanwhile the sun and the clear pebbles of the
>   rain
> are moving across the landscapes,
> over the prairies and the deep trees,
> the mountains and the rivers.
> Meanwhile the wild geese, high in the clean blue
>   air,
> are heading home again.
> Whoever you are, no matter how lonely,
> the world offers itself to your imagination,
> calls to you like the wild geese, harsh and exciting—
> over and over announcing your place
> in the family of things.

Though I think that "the soft animal of your body" is an extremely good phrase, I find the rest of the poem banal. The poem tells you to go easy on yourself, to let yourself love what you love, to see yourself in the world as it goes on around you, to take comfort as the rain falls and the geese fly. You are only you, and all you need (to do) is love (yourself), and even if you're sad and lonely, you can love the wild geese who understand your place in the world, even if you don't. No poem is as balm-like as this one. No poem asks less of you. No poem wants to soothe you through repetition more than "Wild Geese" does. I can see why people love this poem, but it annoys me, in the same way that my mindfulness worksheets from therapy annoy me. Maybe when I am more mindful, I will be less annoyed by being told to look at the geese. Maybe when I am more mindful, I will stop being so judgmental about Gwyneth and spend less time thinking that she should try doing something useful with her obscene wealth and stop trying to sell me jade eggs to put in my vagina. Maybe when I am more mindful, I will like Mary Oliver.

And so I ask myself, when it comes to my corpus of internet poems, why do I like Addonizio's poem and not so much the other three? One reason, I think, is technical. Addonizio's "To the Woman Crying Uncontrollably in the Next Stall," with its heavy enjambments and late volta, is a formally interesting poem. It's not Shakespeare, but it's a poem you can close read. And it's accessible! People get it. This is why I would teach it. The other three poems I've discussed, however, are all free verse poems that aren't particularly interested in doing anything with the freedoms of the form. "A Small Needful Fact," my favorite of the three, uses repetitions effectively, as it constantly stresses its own contingency through conditional words like "perhaps." But that's all I really have to say about its form. For me, someone who knows what poetry can be and do, these three internet poems are a bit blah. They are a bit toothless, a bit politics-less, a bit bland, in content and in form. They are a bit basic, which is exactly why so many people like and share them. They want you to feel better and they might make you feel better! And they might make you feel better by creating a community of other yous to feel better with! Depending on who you are, being encouraged to love yourself might be a radical act. Breathe in the air from the plants, watch the geese fly by, know that your feelings are heard and validated: these poems acknowledge our pain and they want the best for us. These are messages that, abstractly, I can get behind.

They are not for me, though. I prefer the very different types of care that we see in poems by Langston Hughes and Amanda Gorman as well as in many documentary poems. I prefer poems that expose injustices in this terrible world and make demands on it, poems that do not soothe, but seek change. I will take Claudia Rankine over Mary Oliver any and every day of the week. This is an intellectual and aesthetic preference, but also, I have to admit, a personal one, because I have issues. Certain kinds of care, care directed at me, are hard for me to accept. I say this as a white lady with health insurance. In the grand scheme of things, I am fine. But if a poem is going to address me, to insist on caring for me and soothing me, if a poem is going to tell me that things are going to be okay, and if I'm going to believe it, I want it to be carefully crafted messiness for thirteen and a half lines, and then, at the very end, I want it to pause dramatically as one does after a boozy brunch, and say "listen I love you joy is coming" with no banalities about how or when it might come and I want it to come to me by way of a stranger who is halfheartedly drying her hands with a disintegrating brown paper towel on the way of out a public restroom. That is the only way I can stomach hope.

* * *

Rupi Kaur, the bestselling poet in the world, is a poet who people like me love to hate. Her three books— *Milk and Honey* (2014), *The Sun and Her Flowers* (2017), and *Home Body* (2020)—have sold over eight million copies. They have spent years on the *New York Times* bestseller lists and have been translated into forty-two languages. The *New Republic* named Kaur the writer of the decade. You may not know very much about Rupi Kaur, but ask a girl in her late teens or a woman in her early twenties what they think about her poetry. They all have an opinion about Rupi.

Kaur was born in 1992 to a Sikh family in Punjab, India, and immigrated to Ontario, Canada, when she was three years old. What put her on the cultural map, at first, was not her poetry but a school art project. In 2015, when she was a college student at the University of Waterloo, Kaur posted a photo of herself on Instagram lying in bed fully clothed with her back toward the camera. Visible on the sheets and on her sweatpants are two bright stains of menstrual blood. The photo went viral, and Instagram soon took it down for violating its rules. A battle between Instagram and Kaur ensued, and Kaur eventually won, and the photo remains on Instagram today. Kaur's popularity grew exponentially after that photo. People began to read the poems that she had been posting, and she began posting more of them. She had self-published her first book in 2014, and it was soon picked up by Andrews McMeel Universal, which has gone on to publish her other books as well.

Kaur's poems have a distinctive Instagram aesthetic. They tend to be short. They are designed in Times New Roman font and are often accompanied by twee line drawings. Kaur doesn't capitalize any of her words (just as I didn't in my first year of college), includes little to no punctuation, and writes the titles of her poems underneath the body text in italics. Her poems usually have short lines that are broken haphazardly. A recent exemplary Rupi Kaur poem from *Home Body* reads: "it's easy to love / the nice things about ourselves / but true self-love is / embracing the difficult parts / that live in all of us." And, like, true, Rupi. I could not agree with this statement more. It is an accurate statement about emotions: it is hard to love everything about oneself when one is a woman given Society and what it tells us about women and how to be one. It's why I go to therapy. But this poem is barely a poem. It is a sentence broken across five lines for no discernable reason with no discernable effect. Kaur calls her writing poetry, so I am happy to think of it as such, but this poem is basically a sentence out of a self-help book lineated to look pretty on Instagram. Many of Kaur's poems are like this: sentences that make affirmative yet banal statements in clear, accessible language broken across several lines. While not all of them are addressed specifically to girls and women, many of them, such as the poems Kaur writes about her own and others' bodies, explicitly or implicitly are. For example, the poem "you belong only to yourself": "removing all the hair / off your body is okay / if that's what you want to do / just as much as keeping all the hair / on your body is okay / if that's what you want to do." Kaur loves bodily autonomy. Her poems tell us in a million different ways that what you want to do with your body is your choice, whether what you are thinking about doing is shaving or not shaving, masturbating, having sex with someone, whatever.

Beyond messages of self-love and bodily affirmation, Kaur takes on many other topics: sex, intimacy, family, friendship, sexual violence, religion, ethnicity, immigration, origins. Personally, I find Kaur's sex poems to be her cringiest. In a titleless poem, she writes: "i want your hands / to hold / not my hands / your lips / to kiss / not my lips / but other places." In case you think Kaur is being coy, the poem is accompanied by one of her line drawings, an image of the contorted torso and legs of a curvy figure without a face, as if to say: here are the other places you should kiss me. This poem is tame, compared to other poems like this: "the very thought of you / has my legs spread apart / like an easel with a canvas / begging for art." This poem is accompanied by a drawing of an easel. This is the rare rhyming poem in Kaur's oeuvre; the rhyme is so clunky and the simile is so bad that I cannot help but cringe. These poems: they are not good by any metric that I've learned to evaluate poetry by.

But that doesn't mean that they are not valuable. They are incredibly valuable to many, many teenagers. Kaur's poems are not written for people in their thirties like me. Her poems are for people who are newer, people who probably haven't read much if any poetry before, people who are trying to figure out family dynamics and intimacy and body hair and sex, people for whom these things are new and exciting and also probably terrifying. People who might not yet be equipped to think about the politics of bodily autonomy in the national sphere, but who are very much equipped to think about how they are feeling about themselves, people like me at thirteen sobbing on my bed or Kat at the prom or Angela in the boiler room. Kaur's poems, like the other internet poems I've discussed, are poems for everyone in that they are small in their scope. Even when they take on big, political topics, Kaur's poems center the self, your self: your feelings and emotions, your hopes and your fears. Everyone has feelings, even if their form and their content vary greatly, and Kaur is going to affirm the hell out of the fact that you have them whatever they are.

Since it's been a long time since I was an actual young person and part of Kaur's target audience, I decided to talk to a number of high school and college students about the poet. The college students I chatted and texted with spoke about Kaur with a sense of wry detachment. Some of them had followed Kaur on Instagram and bought her books when they were younger, but now they found her to be embarrassing. She was too earnest. She was too mainstream. She had been imitated and memed on social media too much. Liking Kaur was a sign of emotional excess; one college student told me that people her age who still liked Kaur were "depressed, angsty girls." Another told me: "if someone shares a Rupi poem, I know they are really going through something." The word they used over and over again to refer to Kaur was *basic*. These college students also offered compelling critiques of Kaur: of the way she carefully controls her image (should I say here that Kaur is beautiful?), of the way she commodifies her ethnic identity, of the way she attempts to speak for some universal idea of womanhood. These are good critiques. You go to college to learn how to make critiques like this. But mostly, the problem about Kaur is that she is basic: too mainstream, too earnest, too angsty, not self-aware.

When I talked to high school students about Kaur, I heard different stories. One teen told me that she liked Kaur's poems but wasn't particularly attached to them; she told me she sees Kaur's poetry in the same category as the astrology and spirituality accounts that she follows on Instagram and Pinterest. When I asked her who she thinks Kaur's poems are for, if they do not particularly speak to her, she told me, "Rupi is for vulnerable people." I think this is a much gentler version of what I heard from college students: to like Rupi and share her poems is an admission of vulnerability. But the statement itself—"Rupi is for vulnerable people"—almost took my breath away: the directness of it, the lack of condescension. It was not un-Rupi-like, and in a good way.

When I asked another teen—a declared fan of Kaur's—what she thought about the poet, she texted me a long answer:

> Well I liked her enough to write an essay about her in 7th grade saying she was a hero! . . . I've always admired poetry that spills emotions, soul, all of it, and I got that from Kaur's work. A lot of what she writes about is major stuff that I can't relate to (her experiences with SA [sexual assault], racism) but she also has more "minor" things like, if I remember correctly, being a woman—simple romance—domestic life—familial love—respect. These things are interesting to me. I like her writing because I like to see someone put into words what I know I or my friends have been feeling, or even just talking about a subject in a way that lets me see one's thoughts on it. . . . I really think once you look past a bit of the joking around Kaur's style of poetry, she's obviously a great role model.

Putting aside her categories of what counts as major and minor—which could and should be a whole book in and of itself—what stands out to me is the end of this statement. This teen likes Kaur's writing because she can see herself and her friends in it, but also because she can see Kaur writing about a subject "in a way that lets [her] see one's thoughts on it." This is one of the interesting things that poetry can do: it can let you see the thoughts of another human being. Even better when it's not just thoughts, but "emotions, soul, all of it." I started reading books for adults in my adolescence, and I can remember reading them with a purpose, trying to figure out: what are other people thinking about things? Do other people think like I do? Feel like I do? Am I like other people? Am I okay? When I was young, literature was not about the things it is about for me now. Literature was about the chance to peek into other people to see if I was like them.

Of course, one could turn to any form of literature or any writer to ask those questions. Kaur is not unique in that way. But she is the poet who millions of young people have turned to, so she is obviously doing something that is speaking to many, even if only during their adolescence. After years of keeping my eye on her career without ever spending any time with her work, I finally bought and read all of her books and spent a long time scrolling through her Instagram, and I catapulted back and forth between two thoughts: one, these poems are so bad omg, and two, omg I wish I could have read these poems as a teen. Kaur is so candid about love and heartbreak and violence and bodies and relationships. She is so clichéd, but there's a reason clichés are clichés, and when you are fourteen you don't even know the clichés yet, so they don't feel like clichés to you. They just feel good, and right, and true.

I've been reading literature for so long in a critical capacity that I can't remember a time that I ever thought of poets as people who might be "role models," but reading Kaur in light of my conversations with teens, I can't help but think of her this way now. I think Kaur's writing is helpful. I think her Instagram account does important work. I imagine my younger self seeing that viral image of Kaur with the menstrual blood, of reading her poems that affirm *you* even if you are fourteen and messy, even if you are still trying to figure out who you are or might be. Kaur's lack of shame about putting it all out there is embarrassing to older young people who know better, and even embarrassing to me as I read her poems, but enlivening to those who might not yet have developed that particular kind of shame. She's not challenging national narratives, but the structure of feelings she navigates might matter all the same. Kaur models vulnerability and strength and a deep kindness to herself. This is what feels special and different to me about Kaur from any sort of media that I absorbed during my 1990s adolescence: the gentleness that she expresses toward herself and her readers. I am capable of making all of the critiques about Kaur that the college students I spoke with made and more, but the thing is that I just think that these are really good things for teens to read, even if they are pretty bad poems.

One young poet I spoke to felt frustrated that Kaur's bad poems defined the very genre of poetry for her generation, and I understand that feeling. Poetry can be so good! I know just how good it can get! If fourteen-year-olds are into Kaur, imagine what they might think of Amanda Gorman! Or Tommy Pico! Or Morgan Parker! These are highly excellent poets who are also accessible to teens. But the thing is that Gorman's and Pico's and Parker's poems aren't going anywhere. They will be there in a few years, when the teens outgrow Kaur, as many of them seem to do. And if they're lucky, as I was, they will end up in a creative writing workshop, and they will find their poetry weirdos, and they will write their bad poems about oranges and sex and turn bright red when their cute professor talks about their bad poems in class. I hope, too, that they will read poems with more of a political bent, poems that see *you* and your feelings in a larger context, poems that are not so solipsistic, poems that think about peoples rather than just individuals, poems that express care differently. I hope they read poems that demand more from and for them. I want young people to create poetry worlds that include both Rupi *and* Rankine.

Plenty won't; they'll read Kaur and her bad internet poems forever, and write their own tiny bad poems and post them on Instagram, and that will be that. Many of the college students I spoke with talked about how they had written poems when they were teenagers, but that they no longer write them. It's something that teen girls do. And it's hard to write a good poem, but it's easy to write a Rupi-ish poem. I'm glad that Kaur has modeled a form of writing that adolescents can imitate and make their own; not everyone is capable of writing something longer than a five-line poem at fourteen. And you know what, it feels good to write something short and post it on social media and for your friends to like it even if it is bad. It's not about the poem at all, really. Your friends like it because they like *you*. Rupi Kaur made me think about poetry as a genre for beginners: for beginning writers, but beginning people too.

This is a big and silly *if*, but it is an *if* that has been running through my head as I have been reading and writing about Kaur: what if, instead of reading Shakespeare's sonnets and memorizing bits of *Romeo + Juliet*, I had spent my teen years reading poetry by a woman that told me in clear and concise language, language that I could understand, that my body was okay no matter what and that I could do what I wanted with it? That love and sex can be scary and fun all at the same time, that bodies come in all shapes and sizes and that is just how they are, that it is okay to have big messy feelings and even to write about them and want other people to pay attention to them, to pay attention to you? What heartbreaks and aches could I have averted, not so much in my relationships with others, but in my relationship with myself, if I had had Rupi's words to mirror and echo and soothe me? In *Home Body*, Kaur writes: "what a relief / to discover that / the aches i thought / were mine alone / are also felt by / so many others." What if Rupi could have been one of those others for me? I should know better than to think that a book of bad poetry could have changed my life. And yet.

I don't believe in much, but I do believe in poetry. And maybe if I had been born twenty years later, there could have been a version of me who read and loved Rupi Kaur, who grew up to read Mary Oliver without rolling her eyes. Who was maybe a little less anxious, a little more comfortable, a little more okay with being one of those vulnerable people who turns to internet poetry to be soothed and who finds poetry there to soothe her. Someone who does and likes yoga, someone for whom mindfulness training is not full of pain, someone who can handle the kindness of someone else looking at her straight in the eyes and saying "You do not have to be good. / You do not have to walk on your knees / for a hundred miles through the desert, repenting" without cracking a joke about it. Someone who doesn't need her poetry yelled at her from over the wall of a bathroom stall by a person she's never seen. Someone who can just let the soft animal of her body be, and be okay.

CODA

The Villanelle: To Lose

> Oh, must we dream our dreams
> and have them, too?
> —Elizabeth Bishop

When I taught my contemporary American poetry class in Maine, I always looked forward to our day on Elizabeth Bishop's poem "One Art." The poem, probably Bishop's most well-known, is about loss. It takes the form of a villanelle, a French nineteen-line form of poetry built around structured repetitions. "One Art" loosens the traditional villanelle, and Bishop makes subtle changes to the repeating lines to great effect. It is a ruminative form, full of rhymes and echoes and ghosts.

When I would teach "One Art" to my students, we would each take a turn reading the poem aloud. The poem's structure makes it incantatory, and reading it aloud over and over again in a small seminar room around a long table in the late afternoon with snow falling outside created a little electricity in the room, something palpable and crackling. The poem begins:

> The art of losing isn't hard to master;
> so many things seem filled with the intent
> to be lost that their loss is no disaster.
>
> Lose something every day. Accept the fluster
> of lost door keys, the hour badly spent.
> The art of losing isn't hard to master.

The poem, working reversals not dissimilar to those in the sonnets that began this book, meditates on the difficulties of loss and grief but doesn't announce that it's doing so. In fact, it begins by announcing the opposite, that the "art of losing isn't hard to master." The speaker lists things she has lost—a door key, an hour—showing that their loss is no big deal. She commands her audience of readers to follow her in the practice of low-key losing with phrases such as "Lose something every day." Her tone feels assured, almost didactic in these early lines. Loss is easy peasy.

Or so she thinks. The poem continues:

> Then practice losing farther, losing faster:
> places, and names, and where it was you meant
> to travel. None of these will bring disaster.
>
> I lost my mother's watch. And look! my last, or
> next-to-last, of three loved houses went.
> The art of losing isn't hard to master.

> I lost two cities, lovely ones. And, vaster,
> some realms I owned, two rivers, a continent.
> I miss them, but it wasn't a disaster.

As the poem moves forward and the speaker's losses accrue and increase in magnitude, we start to feel as if maybe the speaker isn't being so honest, that actually some losses *are* a big deal. The repetition of the phrases "the art of losing isn't hard to master" and "their loss is no disaster" begin to undermine their surface-level meaning. By the time the speaker tells us that she has lost three houses, two cities (and here is where I start to get teary, at the modifying clause "lovely ones"), a continent, it becomes clear that the art of losing is, in fact, hard to master, even if she hasn't yet admitted it to herself.

Then, the final stanza:

> —Even losing you (the joking voice, a gesture
> I love) I shan't have lied. It's evident
> the art of losing's not too hard to master
> though it may look like (*Write* it!) like disaster.

Oh the last stanza of this poem and how it breaks me, how it has broken me since I first read it in my American poetry class in 2002 when I was still a college student writing my bad poems. The speaker of the poem has been trying to play it cool, but in this final stanza, she cracks. We learn here of her biggest loss, the loss of "you." The address shifts from a generalized "you" to a specific "you," a "you" that has a "joking voice, a gesture / [she] love[s]." The speaker is mourning the loss of a beloved. "One Art," it turns out, is a love poem. And once this beloved is introduced, the repeated phrase "the art of losing isn't hard master" transforms into "the art of losing's not too hard to master." The shift from "losing isn't hard" to "losing's not too hard": well, that shift is everything. It is a quiet admission that this poem so far has been a ruse, that the speaker has been attempting to talk herself into thinking that loss isn't hard to overcome. In the last line of the poem—"though it may look like (*Write* it!) like disaster"—the speaker stages the writing of the poem. She turns inward in the parenthetical and has to command herself to finish the last line and complete the villanelle according to its rules. If she ever believed what she was saying, she doesn't by the end of the poem. The art of losing, actually, is impossible to master, when what's been lost is "you."

* * *

I had a career in poetry and then I lost it. It was a career that I spent most of my adult life working and planning for, making many sacrifices for, building my entire sense of self around. My career was the thing that made me feel like me, the thing that rooted me and helped me to make sense of the rest of the messy world. The loss of my career as a poetry professor has been the cause of the deepest, most profound pain I have ever felt. Poetry is no longer my life's work. I often feel as if I have lost myself.

I have a good job at a university now, a great job even, a job that lets me teach one poetry class per year. I am so lucky, and yet I am still grieving: grieving over a life that I lived with poetry at the center, the life that I might have continued to live in poetry, had many things in academia, in this country, been different.

When I read "One Art" today, I do not just see the grief over the loss of the beloved that I always saw, but I see the aches of the fight against it. I know this struggle from the inside, now: the arguing with yourself, the ruses and rules you create for yourself, the ways you don't want to admit you are (still) grieving when you are. I see the way the repetitiveness of the villanelle form aligns with the repetitive drudgery of grief itself, the echoes and ghosts that pull you back even when you are trying to move forward. This is where I am as a person in 2021. But also, I think, this is where we are as a people in 2021, after the Trump administration but still very much in the throes of late capitalism, with the wildfires burning and the ocean temperatures rising, the COVID-19 pandemic still raging across the world. The losses are still accruing. Still we struggle against them.

I see "One Art," now, as a struggle, and if I do see hope in it, and I'm not sure that I do, it is in the mere completion of the poem, the fact that after the

"(*Write* it!)" still comes the "disaster." The parenthetical command works. The grief is not finished but the poem is. The art of losing this beloved is impossible to master, but still, you go through your motions, you make your rhymes, you complete your stanza, you finish the poem because that is all there is to do.

The beloved is gone but the poetry remains. And that will have to be enough (*Write* it!) for now.

Acknowledgments

Thank you to Sarah Mesle for sliding into my DMs and asking me if I might want to write a book about poetry. You are the most brilliant editor in the world; thank you for teaching me how to write a book. Thank you, too, to Sarah Blackwood for making *Avidly*, which has been such a wonderful home for my writing for years. Thank you to Eric Zinner, Furqan Sayeed, Martin Coleman, and Mary Beth Jarrad at NYU Press and copyeditor Dan Geist for your enthusiasm and skill and for bringing this book into the world.

Thank you to my colleagues Whitney Arnold, Kelly Kistner, Kate McAllister, Veronica Kimaz, and Carolina San Juan for creating a delightful and supportive place to spend my days.

Thank you to my teachers Lee Edelman, Linda Bamber, Lecia Rosenthal, and Peter Richards, who taught me how to read. Thank you to my teachers Michael North, Louise Hornby, Sianne Ngai, Brian Kim Stefans, and Helen Deutsch, who taught me how to think. Thank you to my dear friend Chris Mott for teaching me how to be a teacher.

Thank you to Jeremy Schmidt for being my lifelong comrade in poetry. Thank you to Natalia Cecire,

Megan Cook, Jasmyn Davis, Casey Epstein, Laura Jensen, Nar Peterson, Cole Walsh, Mattie Wyndham, Shayna Yerike, Al Zak, and many others on Twitter who shared poems and feelings with me that I used in this book.

Thank you to the students in my 2020 "Poetry as Resistance" class for helping me think about what poems can do in terrible times. I could not have written chapter 3 without the wisdom of Carlie Abdala, Tabitha Anctil, Megan Anderson, Katherine Barnhill, Jessica Bushman, Matthew Choi, Kristen Comacho, Jamie Dela Cruz, Celia Gleason, Samantha Joseph, Max Kieling, McKenzie Koch, Michelle Lin, Jessa Maheras, Callie Nance, Vivica Rush, Hannah Sitoy, Ashley Takenami, Rachel Teo, Christine Tonione, Felicia Wang, and Minnie Zhang.

Thank you to Gabe Hrynick, Rebecca Colesworthy, Ben Raphael Sher, Cristina Richieri Griffin, Donal Harris, Sarah Tindal Kareem, Sydney Miller, Sonja Thomas, Elisabeth Fairfield Stokes, Laura Levitt, Cliff Davis, Matt Nathanson, Stefanie Todd, Timothy Wagner, Laura King, Jessica Ingram, Caitlin Dean, and Bonnie and James Downing for friendships that have sustained me.

Thank you to Kate Hellenga and Cynthia Rubin Brown for the extraordinary care.

Thank you to Adrian Pellereau and Michael Torsiello for being my LA family.

Thank you to witches Angela Bell, Katie Clonan-Roy, and Chelsea Wessels for being incredibly good to me during my hardest times. And for every cheese plate past, present, and future.

Thank you to my grouptext Ronjaunee Chatterjee, Will Clark, and Amy Wong for being my first and most rigorous readers, my constant virtual companions, and the most hilarious, petty, luminous, and supportive people in my life. This book could not exist without your love.

Thank you to my parents, Diane and David Ardam, and my brother, Eric Ardam, for always believing I could be someone who wrote a book, and for giving me a life in which I could. Thank you to my grandma Marion Tonick, who had two master's degrees, and who always wanted everyone to know.

Finally, thank you to Millie, the world's fluffiest rescue pup, who supervised the writing of every word of this book. You, actually, are the greatest poem.

Works Cited and Consulted

Addonizio, Kim. *Now We're Getting Somewhere: Poems*. New York: W. W. Norton & Company, 2021.

Adorno, Theodor W. "Cultural Criticism and Society." *Prisms*. Cambridge, MA: MIT Press, 1983.

Alam, Rumaan. "Rupi Kaur Is the Writer of the Decade." *New Republic*, December 23, 2019. www.newrepublic.com.

Auden, W. H. *Collected Poems*. New York: Vintage, 1991.

Bishop, Elizabeth. *The Complete Poems, 1927–1979*. Fararr, Straus and Giroux, 2008.

Brown, Kara. "A Conversation with Johari Osayi Idusuyi, the Hero Who Read Through a Trump Rally." *Jezebel*, November 12, 2015. www.jezebel.com.

———. "We Are All This Woman Refusing to Put Down Her Book at a Trump Rally." *Jezebel*, November 10, 2015. www.jezebel.com.

Chaucer, Geoffrey. "An ABC." *Academy of American Poets*. Accessed July 6, 2021. https://poets.org.

Clemmons, Zinzi. "The Role of the Poet: An Interview with Solmaz Sharif." *Paris Review*, July 27, 2016. www.theparisreview.org.

Crain, Patricia. *The Story of A: The Alphabetization of America from the New England Primer to the Scarlet Letter*. Stanford, CA: Stanford University Press, 2000.

Ferguson, Donna. "Poetry Sales Soar as Political Millennials Search for Clarity." *Guardian*, January 21, 2019. www.theguardian.com.

Flood, Allison. "US Poet Defends Reading of Michael Brown Autopsy Report as a Poem." *Guardian*, March 17, 2015. www.theguardian.com.

Gay, Ross. "A Small Needful Fact." *Split This Rock*, April 30, 2015. www.splitthisrock.org.

Gorey, Edward. *The Gashlycrumb Tinies, or, After the Outing*. New York: Harcourt Brace, 1997.

Gorman, Amanda. *The Hill We Climb: An Inaugural Poem for the Country*. New York: Penguin, 2021.

Greene, Roland, Stephen Cushman, Clare Cavanagh, Jahan Ramazani, Paul Rouzer, Harris Feinsod, David Marno, and Alexandra Slessarev. *The Princeton Encyclopedia of Poetry and Poetics*. Princeton, NJ: Princeton University Press, 2012.

Harvey, Matthea. *Modern Life*. Minneapolis: Graywolf Press, 2007.

Hayes, Terrance. *American Sonnets for My Past and Future Assassin*. New York: Penguin, 2018.

Holt, Elvin. "'A Coon Alphabet' and the Comic Mask of Racial Prejudice." *Studies in American Humor* 5.4 (1986): 307–18.

Holzman, Winnie, writer. *My So-Called Life*. "Self-Esteem," season 1, episode 12, dir. by Michael Engler, aired November 17, 1994, ABC.

Hong, Cathy Park. "Delusions of Whiteness in the Avant-Garde." *Arcade*, November 3, 2014. https://arcade.stanford.edu.

Hughes, Langston. *The Collected Poems of Langston Hughes*. Ed. by Arnold Rampersad. New York: Vintage Books, 1995.

"Instapoets Rekindling U.S. Poetry Book Sales, the NPD Group Says." *PR Web*, April 5, 2018. www.prweb.com.

Junger, Gil, dir. *10 Things I Hate about You*. Touchstone Pictures, 1999.

Kaur, Rupi. *Home Body*. Kansas City, MO: Andrews McMeel Publishing, 2020.

———. *Milk and Honey*. Kansas City, MO: Andrews McMeel Publishing, 2014.

———. *The Sun and Her Flowers*. Kansas City, MO: Andrews McMeel Publishing, 2017.

Kemble, E. W. *A Coon Alphabet*. New York: R. H. Russell, 1898. Accessed July 6, 2021. University of Florida Digital Collection. www.ufdc.ufl.edu.

Lorde, Audre. "Poetry Is Not a Luxury." *Sister Outsider: Essays and Speeches*. New York: Penguin, 2007.

Luhrmann, Baz, dir. *William Shakespeare's Romeo + Juliet*, Twentieth Century Fox, 1996.

Martinez, J. Michael. *Museum of the Americas*. New York: Penguin, 2018.

McKay, Claude. *Harlem Shadows*. Brooklyn, NY: Angelico Press, 2021.

Mullen, Harryette. *Sleeping with the Dictionary*. Berkeley: University of California Press, 2002.

The New England Primer. Boston: S. Kneeland and T. Green. 1727. Accessed July 20, 2021. www.bartleby.com.

Oliver, Mary. *Dream Work*. New York: Atlantic Monthly Press, 1986.

Parke, Phoebe. "This Viral Story about a Women Crying in a Bathroom Stall Will Make You Weep." *Grazia Daily*, August 22, 2019. www.graziadaily.co.uk.

Philip, M. NourbeSe. *Zong!* Middletown, CT: Wesleyan University Press, 2008.

Pinsky, Robert. *Jersey Rain: Poems*. New York: Farrar, Straus and Giroux, 2015.

"Poet Billy Collins Reflects on 9/11 Victims in 'The Names.'" *PBS NewsHour*, September 11, 2011. www.pbs.org.

Rankine, Claudia. *Citizen: An American Lyric*. Minneapolis: Graywolf Press, 2014.

Rukeyser, Muriel. *The Book of the Dead*. Morgantown: West Virginia University Press, 2018.

Segal, Corinne. "A Detail You May Not Have Known about Eric Garner Blossoms in Poem." *PBS News Hour*, July 20, 2015. www.pbs.org.

Shakespeare, William. *Shakespeare's Sonnets*. Ed. by Katherine Duncan-Jones. London: Arden Shakespeare, 2003.

Sharif, Solmaz. *Look: Poems*. Minneapolis: Graywolf Press, 2016.

Simpson, David. *9/11: The Culture of Commemoration*. Chicago: University of Chicago Press, 2006.

Smith, Maggie. "Good Bones." *Waxwing*, Summer 2016. www.waxwingmag.org.

Soldier, Layli Long. *Whereas: Poems*. Minneapolis: Graywolf Press, 2017.

Townsend, Hannah, and Mary Townsend. "The Anti-Slavery Alphabet." Philadelphia: Merrihew & Thompson, 1846. www.americanantiquarian.org.

VanRy, Nikki. "Poetry Is More Popular Than Ever, New NEA Research Shows." *Book Riot*. June 7, 2018. www.bookriot.com.

Vendler, Helen. *The Art of Shakespeare's Sonnets*. Cambridge, MA: Belknap Press of Harvard University Press, 1997.

Westminster Assembly. *The New-England primer improved: for the more easy attaining the true reading of English, to which is added, the Assembly of Divines, and Mr. Cotton's catechism*. Boston: Printed for and sold by A. Ellison, in Seven-Star Lane, 1773. Accessed July 6, 2021. www.loc.gov.

Whitman, Walt. *The Portable Walt Whitman*. Ed. by Michael Warner. New York: Penguin Books, 2004.

Woolf, Virginia. *To the Lighthouse*. Orlando, FL: Harcourt, 2005.

"Worlds Collide: Poetry at a Trump Rally." *Rachel Maddow*, November 12, 2015. www.msnbc.com.

About the Author

Jacquelyn Ardam is Assistant Director of the Undergraduate Research Center for the Humanities, Arts, and Social Sciences at UCLA. She lives in East Hollywood with her small dog, Millie.